steady on ...

THE ARTISTS DEVOTIONAL SERIES

steady on ...

... secured by love
point of grace

HOWARD
PUBLISHING CO.

Our purpose at Howard Publishing is to:

- *Increase faith* in the hearts of growing Christians
- *Inspire holiness* in the lives of believers
- *Instill hope* in the hearts of struggling people everywhere

Because He's coming again!

Steady On
© 1998 by Denise Jones, Heather Floyd, Shelley Breen, Terry Jones
All rights reserved. Printed in the United States of America

Published by Howard Publishing Co., Inc.,
3117 North 7th Street, West Monroe, Louisiana 71291-2227

98 99 00 01 02 03 04 05 06 07   10 9 8 7 6 5 4 3 2 1

Library of Congress Cataloging-in-Publication Data

Steady on: secured by love/ Denise Jones... [et al.].
        p. cm. --(The artists devotional series)
    Includes texts of songs performed by Point of Grace.
    ISBN 1-878990-93-4
    1. Devotional literature, English. 2. Contemporary Christian
music--Texts. I. Jones, Denise, 1969-   . II. Point of Grace
(musical group) III. Series.
BV4801.S7 1998
242--dc21   98-35570
                                                                CIP

Interior design by Vanessa Bearden and LinDee Loveland

Dedication . . .

To Cliff Young, for serving us and our ministry
in such a sacrificial way. We love you, brother.

Contents

contents

steady on

x

Acknowledgments

We would like to thank:

Mike Atkins—for your undying dedication to our career.

Philis—you were such an encourager throughout this process. Thank you.

Gary, Denny, and everyone on staff at Howard Publishing—what an incredible pleasure to work with you. Thank you for the opportunity.

The songwriters—for the wonderful devotional inspirations we found in your songs.

steady on . . . .

A man's life is not

his own; it is not

for man to direct

his steps.

—Jeremiah 10:23

Kicking up dust
Heaven or bust
We're headed for the Promised Land
Since the moment we believed, we've
    been eager to leave
Like a child tugging Daddy's hand
May we never forget that patience is a
    virtue
Calm our anxious feet so faithful hands
    can serve you, Lord

(Chorus)
We run on up ahead, we lag behind You
It's hard to wait when heaven's on our
    minds
Teach our restless feet to walk beside You
'Cause in our hearts we're already gone
Will You walk with us

. . . . *steady on* . . . .

We want to walk awhile
We know that every mile is bringing us
    closer home
We want to tell the story
Of sinners bound for glory and turn to find
    we're not alone
When we walk in Your light the lost will
    see You better
As the narrow road gets crowded Lord
    won't You lead us
Steady on

(Chorus)
We run on up ahead. We lag behind You
It's hard to wait when heaven's on our
    minds

Teach our restless feet to walk
   beside You
'Cause in our hearts we're already
   gone
Headed home

(Bridge)
Steady me, when the road of faith
   gets rocky
Oh ready me, for fears I cannot see
Lord won't You let me be a witness
   to Your promise
Won't You steady me

(Chorus)
We run on up ahead, we lag behind
   you
It's hard to wait when heaven's on
   Your minds

. . . *from the album, steady on* . . . .

Teach our restless feet to walk
   beside You
'Cause in our hearts we're already
   gone

(1st Chours)
Will you walk with us
Steady on

Even though it's not easy

to let go, deep down I know

that if I am to have any

stability in my life,

I *must* let God lead.

Heather Floyd

. . . . . *I*t seems as if I'm always in a race with time. Do you ever feel like that? Time is such a fickle master, isn't it? I mean, it's never satisfied. When I was a little girl, I wanted to wear makeup before I was old enough. I wanted to drive before I was old enough. I wanted to grow up before it was time.

When we become adults, the race with time continues. "I have to buy this car before . . . I have to make this much money before . . . I have to have this many children before . . ." *Before what?* What's the urgency? What's the hurry? Why are we so impatient?

We want everything *faster*—quicker microwaves, faster fast food, and shorter shortcuts. Hurry, hurry, hurry! When you buy something that has to be put together, do you ever do what I do—try to put it together without reading the instructions? Reading instructions takes too long; I figure I can do it faster on my own. You'd think I'd learn, though, because every time I try to shortcut the instructions, I experience all kinds of frustration, and the project ends up taking twice as long as it would have if I'd just followed the instructions, step by step.

That's how it is with my life. When I ignore God's instructions and try to do things on my own time, I invariably get myself into trouble. And when I look back on the situation, I see that if I'd just kept in step with God— steady on—things would have turned out much better.

The line in the song "Steady On" that means the most to me is "Teach our restless feet to walk beside you." I don't know about you, but sometimes my feet get mighty restless, and I have a hard time walking *beside* God. Being the human speed-dynamo that I am, I often become impatient with God. I want him to walk at my pace. I want him to do things according to my busy schedule. I want him to answer all my prayers, my way, and on my time. There have even been times in my life when I've tried to answer my own prayers. In essence, I've tried to play God. Guess what happens every time I do that. *Chaos!* Total chaos.

Why is it so hard to do things God's way, at his pace? Why is it so hard to keep in step with him? I think one reason we don't stay steady on our course is that we take our eyes off Jesus. We get distracted. Maybe we even get bored. I love watching Denise's baby, Spence. When someone gets his attention, he looks so intently, so steadily, right in their eyes. He holds his gaze steady . . . until he gets bored, that is. Then he looks around for something more interesting. Aren't we a lot like baby Spence? When life's pace slows, when God's timing takes longer than we'd like, we get bored and wander off on our own.

Another reason we fall out of step with God is that we simply don't trust him. Even though he's told us over and over that he'll take care of us, even though our own life experiences teach us that his way is best, still, our humanity struggles to do things our way. We ignore the teaching of Jeremiah 10:23: "A man's life is not his own; it is not for man to direct his steps." Instead, as the song says, "We run ahead, we lag behind."

We know it's true that we can't see the future like God can, we understand that we don't have the wisdom God has, and it's obvious that we have little power to make good happen. But still, our humanity cries out, "Let me direct my own life!" All the while, God says to us, "Let *me* direct your life. Out of my vision, out of my wisdom, out of my power, out of my compassion and love, let me direct your steps."

Walking steadily beside my God is one of the most terrifying challenges I face in my spiritual life. I have a hard time turning everything over to him, I struggle with trusting him to bring people into my life when I need them, and I wrestle with waiting on him to answer my prayers when I'd rather handle the situation my own way. Even though it's not easy to let go, deep down I know that if I am to have any stability in my life, I *must* let him lead. I pray, to the depth of my being, that my restless feet will learn to walk beside my loving Father, trusting him.

If I can learn to truly trust him, then all my nerve-wracking urgency will fade away. My weak walk will become first steps of faith as I walk "steady on" beside my God, at his direction and in his time.

steady on

questions

1. When was the last time you got impatient with God's timing and struck out on your own? What happened?
2. Have you ever gotten bored with the direction God seemed to be taking you? Did you keep in step with him anyway, or did you get off course? What happened?
3. Recall a time when you trusted God and did things his way even when you were afraid. What did that experience teach you?
4. Are you living your life with heaven in view? If so, how? If not, what needs to change?

. . . steadfast Father,

Teach my restless feet to walk beside you. Forgive me for all the times when I've taken my own course. Guide my feet and light my path. Help me grow in trust so that I'll follow you even when I can't see very far ahead. Help me to run when you run and walk when you walk. Help me keep in step with you.

two

God is with us . . . . . .

Let us fix our eyes on Jesus, the

author and perfector of our faith,

who for the joy set before him

endured the cross, scorning its

shame, and sat down at the right

hand of the throne of God.

—Hebrews 12:2

A rushing river sweeps around us
Just as dark and cold as night, it
  surrounds us
But we pass through the water to
  a safer shore
We're sheltered from the raging
  river's roar

(Chorus)
Though the night is long
And the river's strong
Still God is with us
We can stem the tide
Reach the other side
For . . .

. . . . *God is with us* . . . . . .

The river deepens, night grows darker
And the struggle seems to be
  getting harder
Today has troubles yesterday has
  never known
But we don't have to face them on
  our own

(Chorus)

12

And when we face the river's roll
He holds our hand and won't let go

(Chorus)

. . . *from the album, the whole truth* . . . . . .

When the roar of the waves
in your ears threatens
to drown out the sound of his
voice, listen all the harder.

Denise Jones

. . . . . *d*o you remember when you first learned to swim?

Today, for some reason, my mind slipped back to the summer I learned to swim in deep water. I can almost see the glimmer off the water as the morning sun began to rise to high noon.

During the previous summer, I had learned how to swim in the shallow end, so this summer I'd been moved up to the "advanced class." I was really quite proud to be in the advanced class, but I was also a bit intimidated—I was at least three years younger than everyone else in my class.

Well, on the first day of lessons, my new class met at the deep end of the pool, where the low- and high-dive areas were. My teacher's name was Jenny. She was really sweet and paid special attention to me from the beginning. She called me "half-pint," and she stirred in me a desire to make her proud.

But something happened when it came my turn to swim across the pool. I had done fine swimming the entire length of the shallow pool without touching the bottom, but as stood looking into that deep, dark blue water, I was completely terrified.

Jenny did her best to coax me into the water, but nothing she said made a difference—I just couldn't bring myself to take the plunge. Finally, Jenny got in the water with me and promised that she would swim right alongside of me. With that assurance, I had the courage to try. As long as I kept my eyes on Jenny, I did fine. But as soon as I looked down into the depths of the water, I'd start to panic and begin to dog-paddle. But Jenny never gave up on me. Every day she would get into the water with me and swim alongside of me. If ever I became afraid and started to sink, she was there to get me to the other side.

Finally, on the last day, Jenny sat down beside me at the edge of the pool and said, "Half-pint, I want you to look me straight in the eyes and tell me whether or not you trust me."

"Of course, I trust you, Jenny."

"Have I ever let you go under?" she asked.

"No."

"Okay, then. Today is the day I want you to swim across

the pool all by yourself. I'll stand right over there. And I promise, if you get into trouble, I will jump in that water and bring you to the side. Will you try?"

I knew the time had come; I knew I couldn't keep postponing the inevitable. And I did trust Jenny. She had never let me down, and I knew that she could reach me within seconds if I needed her.

Before I made the dive, Jenny gave me a few last words of encouragment: "Keep your focus on me. You may get tired about halfway, but you'll be fine. Trust me."

When I hit the water, my first reaction was to begin dog-paddling. But I heard Jenny's voice, and I saw her standing across the pool. "You can do it!" she yelled. I began to kick my legs as I had been taught, and I slowly began to breathe as I stretched out my arms, cupped the water, and began to swim. Halfway across, I started to get tired, but I just kept looking at Jenny and knew that she would rescue me if I needed her. I was still one stroke away from the edge when I felt someone take hold of my hand and yank me from the water. It was Jenny, of course. She was so excited that she couldn't wait for me to touch the edge. Thanks to Jenny, I had done it. All I had to do was trust that she would rescue me if needed—and keep swimming.

Do you remember when Peter walked on the water to meet Jesus? He had just seen Jesus feed the five thousand, heal the sick, and do many other miracles. So when Jesus walked across the lake to the disciples' boat, Peter asked Jesus to allow him to walk on the water to meet him. Jesus said, "Come." And Peter went. Can you imagine the thrill Peter must have felt as he stepped on the water and didn't sink? As long as Peter kept his eyes focused on Jesus, he stayed on top of the water. But when he took his eyes off Jesus and began to look at the wind and the waves, he was afraid and began to sink. But, of course, Jesus reached out his hand, caught him, and brought him to safety.

Aren't we a lot like Peter? One minute we believe God is with us and that we can do all things. The next minute a couple of waves rise above our heads, and we take our eyes off of him and focus on the terror around us—and we get scared . . . and we start to sink. All of a sudden, we begin to doubt that the God of the universe can handle our problems.

As you struggle through the waves of life, remember to keep your eyes up and focused on him. When the roar of the waves in your ears threatens to drown out the sound of his voice, listen all the harder. Listen and you will hear him say, "You can do it, _____! I'm right here! You may get a little tired halfway through, but just keep your eyes on me and your ears tuned to my voice, and you'll be all right. And if, for an instant, you begin to sink, I'll be right there to pull you up. I won't let you sink, I promise."

And then when you reach the other side of the stormy waters, he'll yank you up into his arms and tell you how much he loves you and how proud of you he is.

Just keep your eyes on him and keep swimming. He will never leave you.

questions

1. What memories do you have from your childhood about a time when you were afraid to try some new task and someone encouraged you and helped you succeed? What do you remember about the trust you had in that person?
2. What difficult storm have you experienced in your life? Were you able to keep your eyes focused on Jesus, or did you sink like Peter?
3. If you sank like Peter, how did Jesus come to your rescue?
4. Why does keeping our eyes focused on Jesus during a difficult time help us endure?

. . . my Father and my God,

I exalt your glorious name. I praise you for your calming touch in times of trouble. I thank you for your constant presence every day of my life. You are my rescuer, shelter, strength, and comforter. When I find myself in restless waters, I am confident that you will not let me sink. When the roar from troubles fills my ears, I listen for your assuring voice. Help me keep my eyes on you Lord. I don't ever want to lose sight of your face, for in your presence there is no fear.

three

without the love of Jesus . .

Let us then approach the

throne of grace with

confidence, so that we

may receive mercy and

find grace to help us in

our time of need.

—Hebrews 4:16

Some think it all comes down to fate
   and circumstance
Life falls somewhere between accident
   and chance
Some seek solutions to the problems-
   they face
By hoping maybe someday, somehow it
   will all fall in place
We keep persisting
Still something is missing

(Chorus)
Without the love of Jesus
The stars wouldn't shine
Rivers wouldn't run
And hearts beat out of time

. . without the love of Jesus . .

Tell me where would we be?
Lost on a lonely sea
Without the love of Jesus

There's so much more to life than meets-
   the naked eye
It's no coincidence no matter how we try
When we try to deny what we don't
   understand
Maybe that's when we fail to see God's
   providential hand

We keep persisting
Still something is missing

(Repeat chorus)

It shouldn't take us a miracle
Before we finally see
That Jesus' love is the only thing
That we will ever need

(Repeat chorus)

. . . *from the album, the whole truth* . . . . . .

God guides

our hearts and

minds to make

certain decisions

that allow his

love and care

to work.

Shelley Breen

.... *i*t's a mystery to me how God guides our hearts and minds to make certain decisions, but I believe he does.

One afternoon while we were doing a sound check for a concert in North Carolina, we discovered that we had left some important information in Nashville. We always set up a booth for Mercy Ministries at our concerts, and we say something from the stage about the help they give to hurting girls. But on this trip, we had left all the brochures behind. I remember sitting on stage discussing with the girls whether or not we should even mention Mercy Ministries. Without the brochures and the envelopes for collecting donations, we didn't know if it would be worth the effort. However, for no particular reason that I can remember, we decided to go ahead and have Denise share from the stage what Mercy Ministries is all about.

What we didn't know was that there was a young girl in the audience that night who desperately needed to hear about God's mercy, and she needed to hear it quickly. Just that day, she had found out that she was pregnant. Unmarried and a teenager, I'm sure she felt her situation was insurmountable.

As Denise shared about Mercy Ministries that night, the Holy Spirit did a work in that young girl's life. After the concert, she came through the autograph line and inconspicuously asked for Mercy's Special Help Line (1-800-922-9131). We don't even remember her asking!

We later found out that the very next morning she placed a call to Mercy Ministries. She told them she was about to have a secret abortion but that she had heard from us that there was a place she could go to find help and hope without being judged for her past mistakes. It makes me shudder to think that we almost didn't share about the ministry because of some stupid brochures! This girl chose to come to Mercy Ministries here in Nashville, and praise God, her baby was saved and she got her life together with God's help.

I have to believe that without the love of Jesus, this never would have happened. The story wouldn't have had a happy ending. But because he cared for that little girl in that small North Carolina town, he reached down from heaven and made a way, when to her, there seemed to be no way.

So when people try to say that it all comes down to fate, we as Christians need to be the voice that says it all comes down to the love of Jesus. It's a mystery to me how God guides our hearts and minds to make certain decisions that allow his love and care to work. And even though I don't understand it, I believe I saw the divine providence of God at work that night. And you can believe that his providence is at work in and through your life too.

The song says, "Some think it all comes down to fate and circumstance, life falls somewhere between accident and chance," but if we believe that the God of the universe orders the universe and orders our steps, we know that in reality "it's no coincidence."

questions

1. How has God intervened in your life to give you just the help you needed just when you needed it?
2. Who has God worked through to bless you?
3. Who has God blessed through you?
4. What's the difference between fate and providence? What do you believe is working in your life?

. . . my Father in heaven,

Help me to be open to your Spirit so that you can bless others through me. Open my eyes to see your work all around me, and help me submit to your work in me. Forgive me for the times that I subconsciously attribute your work to fate. I praise you for caring enough about each and every one of us that you reach down from heaven and move in our lives.

four

my God . . . .

Consider it all joy, my brothers, when

you encounter various trials, knowing

that the testing of your faith produces

endurance. And let endurance have its

perfect result, so that you may be

perfect and complete, lacking in nothing.

—James 1:2–4 NASB

All my life You have been with me
How could I pretend not to see
I was walking on the line
I was wasting precious time
All I know is that You love me
If I call You will set me free
It's a promise that You made
It's the truth that will not change
Please help me to remember

(Chorus)
My God has never let me down
My God has turned my world around
He loves me even though I know I don't
   deserve Him
My God has never turned away
He's with me every single day

. . . . *my God* . . . .

He's broken all the chains and set this
   captive free
Seems to you all your hope is gone
Never found a love that strong
It's a chance you have to take
A choice you've got to make
I hope that you'll remember

(Chorus)
My God will never let you down
My God can turn your world around

He loves us even though I know we
    don't deserve Him
My God will never turn away
He's with you every single day
He's broken all the chains and set
    this captive free

(2nd Chorus)

(1st Chorus)

(2nd Chorus)

Set this captive free

. . . from the album, steady on . . . .

MY GOD. Words and music by Carla Sullivan ©1996
New Car Tunes/Landyman Music/BMI

I cling to God, not because it is the trendy thing to do, but because I know I can't live without his direction in my life.

Terry Jones

. . . . . . *t*o look at me now, you'd never know what I've been through. You might think everything is and always has been easy for me. But there's a side of me not everyone knows. There's a side of me that's had a lot of experience with a father in prison. I know what it's like to drive six hours to a prison once a month to see your dad. I know how it feels to spend holidays with your father in a smoky, drab room, with twenty or so other families trying to share some holiday cheer around cafeteria-style tables. I can tell you how it feels to picture your dad standing in a long line, waiting his turn to get to a phone to make his daily phone call home. I could explain the pain of hearing your father's verdict of guilty in a courtroom after years of trials. I know all this because I lived it—twice.

It happened for the first time when I was in the fourth grade. My all-American, devout Christian, loving, great daddy was sent to prison for four months. The prison was six hours from our house, and we would make the drive one weekend a month. He was sent to prison on charges regarding his business. He was the president of a great company, but got involved in a bad deal.

At the time, we lived in the nicest country club in town, Mom and Dad had Porsches, and we had a vacation home in a ski resort and enough money to live well and take great vacations to Europe. But it doesn't take long for all of this to disappear when your father is sent to prison. We had to pay an enormous sum of money to the government—all we had and then some. To put it mildly, we lost more than pride. But through it all, my dad's enduring faith was an example to our entire family and helped us remain strong.

When my dad was released from prison, my parents' marriage was still intact, which was a miracle considering that every other person we knew in prison was divorced. We were so grateful, now, for our family's together time. We moved to Oklahoma for a new start with what my parents thought was a great company. But it happened again. The government did a "sting" type investigation on this new company and, although what they found happened before Dad got there, he was roped in and found guilty by association.

The courts aren't too easy on someone who has a prison record, and this time he was sent to prison for five years. I was a junior in high school at the time, and having a father in prison was not an easy thing for an insecure high schooler to handle. Dad's new "home" was in a minimum security prison about an hour and a half away from home. At least he was closer this time, and we went up to see him as often as possible.

It was all so unfair. I struggled not to get bitter at the judge and attorneys who put my father in prison. Mom, me, and my three sisters tried to live as normally as possible, even though we really didn't have anything. But God was faithful to provide for us, and he comforted us when life seemed too much to bear. We didn't have money to pay for haircuts, so a sweet hairdresser friend cut our hair for free. Kind people brought us food for the holidays, and checks would just show up in the mail to help us pay bills. Mom took a job at the church, and somehow, Mom and Dad's strength held us together.

The day I graduated from high school was one of only two days that year that Dad got furlough and was able to be with us. The other day was Christmas. When I went off to college, I had a hard time knowing how to answer questions about my dad and my family. I didn't want to hide the truth, but it was very difficult to explain the whole story and not be misunderstood. It was not something that most people in that little Baptist college could relate to.

This experience was the most difficult I've ever lived through. I still get very emotional when I think about it. But now, when I look back, I can clearly see the lessons I learned through that ordeal and wouldn't change what happened—except to take away the pain my dad and mom felt. But as for my pain, it gave me perspective. I learned the difference between what is important in life and what is not worth worrying about.

I learned that grabbing on to Christ and his Word was important. I learned that our family's staying together was imperative. And I learned that having only $1.50 to buy lunch was not all that important. I had to grow up and be responsible—something that some people never do—and I am glad I had to learn it younger than most. That experience made me so grateful for the tiniest of things, like watching my mom and dad together at home or having enough money to buy that special dress or the freedom and ability to go and do what I want.

I have spent many sleepless nights crying so hard I thought I would never stop, but I have come out on the other side, and I can see that a mighty hand was at work in me to show me that he has great plans for my life. I cling to God, not because it is the trendy thing to do, but because I know I can't live without his direction in my life.

Some of you may look at my life and say, "God really let her down." But I would answer with an absolute "No!" I was able to learn so much more than most people, and he brought my family out of the mire and into a wonderful life. I would say,

My God has never let me down
My God has turned my world around
He loves me even though I know I don't deserve
    Him
My God has never turned away
He's with me every single day
He's broken all the chains
And set this captive free

By the way, my parents have a pretty cool story to tell about what God has done for them too. When my dad was released, their marriage remained strong, and they now work together in a prison ministry, encouraging prisoners to follow God. They know how to relate to the hurt they see daily.

Isn't God amazing how he turns our worlds around for his purposes?

questions

1. Is there anything sad about you that most people don't know? Can you see God's hand in this situation? Can you feel his comfort?
2. Has anything happened to you that seems totally unfair, something that tempts you to become bitter? Will you dare trust God to work "everything together for good"? (Rom. 8:28).
3. What specific lessons have you learned from the pain you've faced so far in your life?
4. After reading this devotional, has your idea of what's truly important changed? How?

. . dear God who never lets me down,

Thank you for walking with me through the pain of this life. But sometimes I hurt so badly that I can't see anything good. Please ease my pain and open my eyes to see your plan for me. Help me not to blame you for the hard times but to blame the true source of pain—Satan. Help me be brave while I endure. I praise you for bringing me through past difficulties, and I praise you in advance for bringing me through future pain.

five

faith, hope & love . . . . .

In my distress I called to

the Lord; I called out to

my God. From his temple

he heard my voice; my

cry came to his ears.

—2 Samuel 22:7

(Chorus)
Faith, hope and love
Is more than enough when times get tough
Faith, hope and love
Will tunnel through what's in front of you
If you just trust in faith, hope and love

There's a lot of things we face
That seem to pull us down
There's a lot of tears and pain
That turn our world around
Seems the hammer always falls against us
At our weakest times
But I know a power that can heal
The wounds it leaves behind
It's a stone's throw away
From anything we may face

(Chorus)

. . . . . faith, hope & love . . . . .

Is more than enough when times get tough
Faith, hope and love
Will tunnel through what's in front of you
If you just trust in faith, hope and love

There's a lot of hurt and sorrow
That can cloud the bluest skies
Still there's hope in tomorrow
If we just close our eyes
To every fear we must face
As we learn to embrace

(Chorus)
You can trust
You can really, really trust
In faith, hope and love

(Bridge)
Just a little faith will pave the road
   before you
To see you through

(Chorus 3x)

. . . *from the album, point of grace* . . . .

God knew

the exact moment

I needed his hand

to gently stroke

my head and fill

my heart with

peace.

Heather Floyd

. . . . . *i* have never been so stressed in my entire life. I'm buying my first house. Need I say more? Through the years, I moved many times with my family, but I never really paid attention to the process. I was too busy wondering which room would be mine. I just assumed that buying a house would be a breeze. I'll find the right house, buy some new furniture, get some guys to move my stuff, and I'll be set. *Not!* I was in for the shock of my life. Nothing went as planned.

Just the other day I was driving down I-65 feeling overwhelmed and all bogged down by all the piddly decisions I was having to make. Fifteen- or twenty-year mortgage? Fixed or variable rate? Hardwood or carpet, black or white appliances? And what day can I squeeze the closing into my schedule? *Yikes!* Calgon, take me away!

All these thoughts were flooding my mind, and I felt extremely alone. I never thought I'd be making these decisions alone, and I couldn't stand the way it was making me feel. To be painfully honest, I was out of control. Just when I felt my head was about to explode, something incredible happened. I felt an overpowering sense of God's presence. I was intensely aware that "faith, hope, and love is more than enough when times get tough." I was completely filled, head to toe, with an unexpected, wonderful peace. I didn't ask for it—I didn't have the presence of mind to ask for it—but suddenly, as I passed the Brentwood Skating Rink, the peace that passes understanding surrounded me. I could feel it in every fiber of my being. God's gentle peace. Calm in the midst of life's little storm. I was not alone. God was right there with me in my car. My sovereign God knows every thought, and my sovereign God knew the exact moment I needed his hand to gently stroke my head and fill my heart with peace. When I finally acknowledged his almighty presence, I could find no words to express my gratitude to him. I just cried. My nose started to sting and tears poured from my eyes. The God of everything went out of his way to allow me to experience his presence.

Several weeks later, my parents came to help me move. One morning, as we were taking care of some final details,

I came all undone again. My precious mother recognized the stress in my eyes. She went to her Bible and pulled out a little piece of paper. "Honey, I know I've read this to you before, but let me read it to you again." It was an excerpt from one of her devotionals. It said,

> God is relaxed. God's timing is perfect. God has continuous energy. God is in control. God knows everything. This God is living in me. He is working through me.

One more time, I cried. Through my sweet mother, God reminded me that I am his and he is mine. The God of the universe, the creator of all things, really does care for me. And then, a few days later, I was sitting outside and a tiny bird landed next to me. It had an enormous piece of bread in its beak, and I wondered, Where in the world did that little bird find such a big piece of bread?

Then I realized that this little bird didn't worry about where his food came from. It simply trusted that God would provide. If such a big God cares about the birds of the air, how much more does He care for me? As I contemplated these thoughts, the words of an old song by Civilla D. Martin came to mind:

> Why should I feel discouraged? Why should the shadows fall?
> Why should I be lonely and long for heaven and home?
> Jesus is my portion, my constant friend is He.
> His eye is on the sparrow, and I know He watches me.

questions

1. What stresses you out the most? When was the last time you felt stressed?
2. Where is your focus when you feel stressed? How can shifting your focus to God make a difference?
3. Have you ever experienced God's peace as described in this devotional? What were the circumstances? What did you learn from the experience?
4. How can God living in you help you to accomplish things you could not accomplish on your own?

. . dear God of peace,

Sometimes I get so wrapped up in my problems that I lose all sense of your presence. Forgive me for taking my eyes off you and focusing on the things of the world. When you see me doing this, please pull me back into your presence. Do whatever it takes to get my attention. Thank you for the gift of peace that you so freely fill me with, even when I am distracted and overwhelmed—especially when I am distracted and overwhelmed. I praise you for the peace of your presence.

six

love enough . . . .

My grace is

sufficient for you,

for my power is

made perfect

in weakness.

—2 Corinthians 12:9

On your own
All alone and crying
A wounded soul on an island in the blue
Love's required
But you're so tired from trying
Don't give up
There's love enough for you

(Chorus)
There's love enough for a broken heart
Love enough for another start
Love enough in the Father's arms for you
When it feels like the tears won't end
When loneliness is your only friend
There's love enough
Love enough for you

. . . . *love enough* . . . . .

On His own
All alone and dying
He gave up everything for me and you
Hear your heart
It's time to start relying
On the One who had love enough for you

(Chorus)

Like a cup that's running over
Like a well that won't run dry
From the storm a constant cover
For a heart, the sole supply

(Chorus 2x)

Love enough for you
Love enough, love enough
Love enough for me
Love enough for you

. . . from the album, point of grace . . . .

LOVE ENOUGH. Words by Robert Sterling and music
by Scott Williamson ©1993 Word Music (a div. of Word,
Inc.) (ASCAP)

God wrapped his big arms around me and touched my heart where it hurt.

Denise Jones

*L*ife was perfect. Our precious new baby was three weeks old and a constant marvel. Our home was everything I'd always wanted, complete with a white picket fence and a golden retriever. And our marriage was happy and growing. Although I was recovering from a difficult delivery and wasn't getting enough sleep (what new mom does?), I felt as if I could accomplish anything. The world was at my feet, and I was happily in control.

On this particular day, Point of Grace had been working in the studio to complete our fourth album. Stu was home taking care of Spence and being the perfect "Mr. Mom." We'd finished recording later than usual, so as I left the studio I called home to let Stu know I was on my way. An unexpected voice answered the phone. It was Karri, my neighbor. She quickly informed me that baby Spence was fine, but there was something wrong. My dog, Freethrow, had been hit by a car.

If you know anything about Point of Grace, you know that we are dog fanatics. Freethrow had become a part of my and Stu's family on our first wedding anniversary. He had the sweetest temperament and was now four years old. Everyone loved Freethrow.

As I drove home, I had a sick feeling in my stomach. How badly had Freethrow been hurt? Was he even alive? Was he in pain? Would surgery help? As I drove, I begged God to let him live. You see, I had everything all planned out . . . Spence and Freethrow were going to be best buddies. When Spence was old enough, they would play ball and go on walks and even sleep together.

When I pulled into the driveway, Stu met me outside—without Freethrow. He had died on the way to the veterinarian. We cried together for at least an hour while Karri held Spence in the next room.

I know that losing a dog is a minor thing compared to all the pain in the world. But at that moment, I really hurt. I was a new mom, dealing with new responsibilites; Point of Grace had just finished our first day back in the studio, and it had been a long one; all my hormones were bouncing around like thousands of out-of-control Ping Pong balls—and now I'd lost my sweet puppy! It all hit me that night in the middle of Spence's two o'clock feeding. I sat all alone in my brand new glider rocker, holding my innocent, unaware infant, and cried my eyes out.

Through my tears, my heart cried out to my heavenly Father, "Lord, I can't do this! This is too hard. Why did this have to happen now, when everything was perfect, when everything was just as I'd planned?" And softly, the answer came almost immediately, "My grace is sufficient for you, for my strength is perfected in weakness." Like a soothing wash over my soul, I felt God's gentle presence. He reminded me that I was right—I couldn't do this—not without his help. Life is not meant to be perfect, we are not meant to stand alone on our own strength. In our weakness, God shows his strength; when we are afraid, he is our stronghold.

I learned something that day about pain, and I learned something about control. Of course, the pain of losing a puppy is nothing compared to what so many suffer. When a young wife discovers that her husband, the love of her life, has been unfaithful to his marriage vows, she feels deep, gut-wrenching pain. When a wife and child are killed in a car wreck, that husband and father's pain is undescribable. Or when the doctor says "malignant," feelings of fear and desperation fill the heart. Everything can be going along exactly as we want it to, and *wham!* all of a sudden our life is spinning out of control and it *hurts!* You can hurt so badly and so deeply that your soul aches and your heart almost bursts under the weight. Your pain can be so bad that you don't want to get up in the morning because you just don't think you can face the day. And it seems that surely no one can understand how you feel.

But since that night, I've gained new insights into 2 Corinthians 12:9—the verse that came to me as I cried in my rocker. I've learned that the original Greek language this verse was written in can be translated into English as "My influence on your heart and my reflection on your life is enough for you, for my strength is perfected in your weakness." Isn't that a beautiful rendition? Because of our relationship with God, his spirit has influence over our lives. He is big enough to reach down to the bottom of our souls and love us like no one else can.

That night, sitting alone with Spence, I found God's peace. He wrapped his big arms around me and touched my heart where it hurt. And I think in some small way, I am now better prepared to handle bigger pains.

You, my friend, may be hurting too. Your heavenly Father will help you look at life the way he sees it. Life is not always what we expect, but if you will let go and let God reach into your heart and open your eyes, you will see that he is right beside you and that his big, strong arms are wrapped securely around you. You can know that he will never leave you, that he will never let you down.

Remember, God knows what pain is. What greater pain could there be than watching your own son die—and he allowed it to happen for you and me. Don't you think it's time to rely on him? His abundant showers of grace and love are more than enough.

questions

1. When was the last time something bad happened and took you by surprise? What happened? What did you learn from the experience?
2. How do painful experiences help us to focus on and trust in God's love?
3. What is the most emotionally painful experience you've ever had? Were you able to lean on God's love during the pain? If not, how can you handle your next painful experience differently so that you can draw strength from God?
4. When you think of the pain that God suffered while he watched his own Son die, how does that give you strength to endure your own heartache?

. . . . *loving Father,*

Help me look to you when I hurt. Whether the pain is little or big, remind me that I can come to you for comfort. Help me to see my pain in perspective and to know that "this too shall pass." Thank you for loving me so much that you endured the pain of letting your sinless Son die for sinful humanity.

seven

more than anything . . . . .

Neither height nor depth, nor

anything else in all creation,

will be able to separate us

from the love of God that is

in Christ Jesus our Lord.

—Romans 8:39

(Chorus)
God loves people more than anything
God loves people more than anything
More than anything He wants
   them to know
He'd rather die than let them go
'Cause God loves people more
   than anything

God loves the weary
When they're too weak to try
He feels their pain, He knows their shame
He cries with those who cry
He won't give up or walk away
When other people do
'Cause God loves people . . .

. . . . more than anything . . . .

(Chorus)

God loves the wounded
Who've stumbled into sin
He reaches down and pulls them out
And cleans them off again
And He will heal the broken heart
That's given up on love
'Cause God loves people more
   than anything

(Chorus)

More than anything He wants us
  to go
And show the world so they will
  know
That God loves people more
  than anything

. . . *from the album, the whole truth* . . . .

You were designed

by Jesus Christ,

and, yes, he loves you

more than anything—

and that's enough.

Shelley Breen

. . . . . *P*oint of Grace was once given a great piece of advice: Never speak to an audience (or to anyone else, for that matter) beyond your own experience.

Well, seven years ago when we first came together as Point of Grace, fresh out of college, we didn't feel we had much to share. We were young and inexperienced, and we hadn't encountered much of "life." But one thing we had experienced was the *love of God*. And with every passing year, we come to know his love even more. I guess that's why that theme runs throughout our concerts.

It may seem like a simple concept, and in many

ways, I guess it is; but in reality, our need to be loved is one of our strongest emotional longings. We want to be loved just about "more than anything." When you're feeling bad about yourself or left out and alone, what you crave is affirmation and acceptance. And where do we usually look for this affirmation and acceptance? We most often look to other people—kids at school, coworkers, family members, or people at church. And often times, we do get love and acceptance from these people . . . but not always and not enough.

While Point of Grace is on the road, we meet so many young girls and guys who feel they don't quite measure up. Maybe they think they're not smart enough, not pretty enough, or not funny enough. Whatever they feel is lacking, it's always measured by what other people think and not what God thinks. I wish these kids would understand that they are loved by the Creator of the universe, by the Savior of the world!

I want to tell them, "Who cares? Who cares if you're not the most popular or if you don't have the so-called coolest clothes. You were designed by Jesus Christ, and, yes, he loves you more than anything—and that's enough." As God's children, we can hold our heads up high, knowing that our identity comes from God. He created us just the way we are—on purpose—and he has a plan for our lives.

But how can we come to understand God's love for us? First and foremost, we must remember what he did for each individual person—that means me and that means you—by allowing his Son to die on the cross. The Bible tells us that we are sinners and that the wages of sin is death. In this case, death means the presence of hell and the absence of heaven, for all eternity. But God, because of his love for us, didn't want us to endure what we deserve. And so he sent his only Son to die as a sacrifice for me and for you. That God would do this for us proves beyond a shadow of a doubt that he really does love people more than anything.

Another way that God shows his love to us is through the peace he gives us. I don't know about you, but I'm a very worried and stressed-out person most of the time. On a daily basis, it seems, I find a million things to fret about. Often, when I'm driving in my car or alone with my thoughts, my mind begins to fill with all sorts of concerns. One worry leads to another, and in five minutes my peace with myself and with God is completely gone. I've been challenging myself lately to remember that life is short, that none of the things I'm worrying about really have any eternal consequence, and that God loves me more than anything. When I think on these things, most always, he calms my mind and brings me peace. I am assured of his love because I see that he cares for my smallest concerns, my irrational worried thoughts, and replaces them with comfort, love, and peace.

"More than anything"—that means that to God nothing comes before us. My own priorities often get way out of whack, but God's never do. In every circumstance, no matter what we are going through, we can be assured that God loves us more than anything.

I have found that when I ask God to comfort me with the assurance of his love that he faithfully honors that request. In God's love is where you find self-worth and confidence, not to mention the most significant love of your life.

questions

1. How have you experienced God's love in your life?
2. What makes you feel bad about yourself? How can being aware of God's love for you make you feel better?
3. What do you worry and stress about? Have you ever asked God to replace your worries with peace and comfort? What has been the result?

God of peace and comfort,

Please help me to be aware that you really do love me more than anything. I praise you for being the kind of God who uses his power to work good and not harm in my life. Help me turn to you when I need assurance and affirmation. Forgive me when I allow other people's standards to determine my self-worth.

eight

who am i? . . . .

How great is the love

the Father has lavished

on us, that we should

be called children of

God! And that is

what we are!

—1 John 3:1

Over time You've healed so much in me, I
am living proof
That although my darkest hour had come,
Your light could still shine through
Though at times it's just enough to cast a
shadow on the wall,
Well I am grateful that You shine Your light
on me at all

Who am I . . . that You would love me so
gently?
Who am I . . . that You would recognize
my name?
Lord who am I . . . that You would speak
to me so softly?
Conversation with the love most high . . .

. *who am i?* . . . . . .

Amazing grace how sweet the sound that
saved a wretch like me,
I once was lost but now I'm found, was
blind but now I see,
And the more I sing that sweet old song,
the more I understand,
That I do not comprehend this love that's
coming from Your hand . . .

Who am I . . . that You would love me so
gently?
Who am I . . . that You would recognize
my name?
Who am I . . . that You would speak to me
so softly?

Conversation with the love most
   high . . . who am I?
Grace, grace God's grace
Grace that will pardon and cleanse
   within,
Grace, grace, God's great grace,
Grace that is greater than all my sin

Who am I . . . that You would love
   me so gently?
Who am I . . . that You would
   recognize my name?
Lord, who am I . . . that You would
   speak to me so softly?
Conversation with the love most
   high . . . who am I?

. . . . *from the album, steady on* . . . .

Lord who am I?
Who am I?
Who am I?

WHO AM I? Words and music by Nathan and Christy
Nockles © 1998 Sweater Weather Music/BMI

C

Can you picture God

lovingly shaping you,

carefully putting

your pieces

together?

Terry Jones

. . . . . *A*s I write this, I am one month away from having a baby—my first. The realization that God has created a whole new person and that person is growing inside of *me* fills me with awe and a deep sense of responsibility.

I know so little about this child. I don't know if it's a boy or girl (we decided to be surprised). I don't know what color its hair will be, whether it will like green peas, or whether it will be outgoing and athletic or shy and creative. Will our child love to sing, like me, or play basketball, like Chris. Will he or she grow up to be a business accountant or an interior decorator?

The other day I was watching television and I saw Shawn Colvin on *The Rosie O'Donnell Show*. Shawn was five months pregnant at the time, and as she was talking about her pregnancy, she said, "We know that someone new is coming to live with us, to move in, but we don't even know his or her name." I know exactly how she feels! Chris and I can hardly believe that we will have a new person in our lives in such a short time—a person whom we know nothing about.

And besides being so amazed that I know so little about this person inside me, I feel overwhelmed with the responsibility of properly caring for and raising this child. As an elementary education major in college, I student taught kindergarten and third grade. I loved teaching these sweet children, but I was saddened to see so many who were unloved and uncared for. There were five-year-old children in my class who would take the bus home and let themselves in to an empty house. One little girl had a mom who was a prostitute. As their teacher, I loved these children as best I knew how, but when they went home at 2:30, they were on their own. Seeing this neglect made me all the more committed to be a responsible, caring mommy when I had children.

As I think about the wonder and the responsibility of being a parent, I can't help but think about God as my parent. God is many things to us: He is Lord, he is King, he is Creator, and so much more. But my favorite thing that God is to me is *Father*. When I think about God and how powerful and majestic he is, I sometimes have a hard time understanding how he could care about insignificant me. "Who am I that he would love me so gently? Who am I that he would recognize my name?" But then I remember that I am his *child.* And that helps me understand just a little of how he could love me. Because when our baby is born, it won't matter what it looks like or what personality it has. It won't matter what special abilities and talents it has or doesn't have. We will love this baby unconditionally and forever just because it's ours. For no other reason than it's ours.

And that's why God loves you. Just because you're his.

The Bible says that before you were even born, God created your inmost being and knit you together in your mother's womb (Psalm 139:13). Can you picture God lovingly shaping you, carefully putting your pieces together? Can you see him "knitting" each cell and each chromosome just so. God knows how many hairs are on your head. He knows everything about you. He even knows your name.

As Chris and I wait anxiously for our baby, it's comforting to know that although we know so little about our new child, God knows everything! He knows how many hairs are on its little head; he knows what color eyes it will have; he knows who his or her best friend will be in the second grade; he even knows if its belly button will be an "innie" or an "outie."

I can't wait to begin loving our new child. It is our prayer that our son or daughter be *surrounded* by unconditional love—mommy and daddy love, gramma love, aunt love, friend love, and of course God's huge, out-stretched love. And it is our prayer that our child will know who he or she is in Christ, that "He would love our child so gently, that he would recognize his or her name."

Who am I? I am now a mommy, with all the responsibilities and joys that come with it. God so gently holds me, he so gently cares for my baby. Who are we? We are loved *so* deeply. We are his little babies.

questions

1. What is your favorite thing that God is to you? Lord? Savior? Father? Why?
2. What about you is unique? Why do you think God created you with those special characteristics? How can you use them for God?
3. Do you ever have difficulty believing that God could love you? Why? How does thinking of yourself as God's *child* help you comprehend his love?
4. What is unconditional love? Why is that kind of love better than conditional love?

. . . *my Father in heaven,*

It is so good to be able to call you that. You are the perfect Father. You have lavished me with love, directed me away from danger, and showered me with blessings. You knew me before I even existed, and you loved me even then. You have placed a spiritual ring on my finger and given me your name and the life of your Son. I will never understand why you feel such devotion to any person, but I am filled with gratitude that you have made me yours. If someone should ask who I am, I will tell them I am my Father's child. That will say it all.

take me back . . . .

I am the light of the

world. Whoever

follows me will

never walk in dark-

ness, but will have

the light of life.

—John 8:12

Been too long chasing selfish dreams
Seeking only what my heart desired
I've drifted so far away it seems
From the truth that set my soul on fire
How many times will it take for me to see
That You're the only love my heart will
    ever need?

(Chorus)
Take me back, take me back, Jesus
Take me back
To where I can know Your love
Take me back, take me back, Jesus
Take me back
Won't you take me back
Take me back, take me back, Jesus

. . . . *take me back* . . . . . .

To where I can feel Your love
Take me back, take me back, Jesus
Take me back

Like the Prodigal far from home
Lost inside a world of my own choosing
Tried to make it out on my own
Never realized all I'd be losing
I still remember, just how it used to be
Lord, forgive my weakness
Come and rescue me

(Chorus)
There's no one else I would turn to
You're the only one who can pull
  Me through
You can pull me through

(Chorus)

. . . . *from the album, the whole truth* . . . .

I've taken many wrong turns

and a few detours,

but I always find

my way back

to the narrow road.

Heather Floyd

. . . . . *i* am on a journey—an exciting, adventurous journey. It's a journey on the road of life. Along my journey I experience thrills and spills, and I encounter enormous mountains and vast valleys.

I've taken many wrong turns and a few detours, and I've lost my way in the wilderness countless times. But, somehow, I always find my way back to the road, the narrow road. My Master keeps it all lit up for me so I'll always be able to find my way home.

You know how on hot summer nights, you can see the lights of a softball field all the way across town? Even if it's a long way off, if you'll follow the lights, you can eventually find your way to the field. God's light is like that. It penetrates the darkness and shines steadfastly, and if you'll just keep it in view and keep making your way toward it, you'll eventually end up right there with him.

But sometimes, the freedom of the wide road seems much more fun than the confines of the narrow road. And I find myself wandering off course and away from God. On the wide road, I can make my own rules and decide my own way. And I like that . . . for a while. But soon the air there becomes bitter and stale. And the crowds of people press against me, and I get sweaty and covered in dust. I begin to feel as if I'm suffocating. And it's so dark, and I feel so lonely—even though I'm surrounded by thousands of other lost souls. And in my desperation, I begin to frantically search for the light. I finally spot it, but it's far away, and I'm tired and weary. I want to give up and rest right where I am. But I know that could get me in trouble. It's sort of like sleeping in your car at a rest stop in the middle of nowhere. Anything can happen.

I'm so tired and so far from home, and I've accumulated so much baggage that I can't possibly carry it all on my own. I've been away from the light so long that I've forgotten that there are people there who really want to help, and that there is One who is strong and loving and wants to carry my load. He misses me and wants me to come home.

But I'm so ashamed. I've turned my back on him; I can't ask him for help now. I can't go home. Just look at me. My face is smudged with dirt, my clothes are filthy and worn, my hair is wild and out of control—just like my life. My body is covered with cuts and bruises, and I know they're there because of my own stupid choices.

I can't go home . . . not like this. I look again at my sad surroundings, then I lift my face to the magnificent road in the distance, all lit up and waiting for me. I know I want to go there; I want to experience the warmth of the light once again. Just then, I hear a faint noise coming from far down that luminous road. The sound gets louder and louder, and it sounds so beautiful—like someone cheering and joyfully clapping and shouting. Then I hear my name. I can't believe it. Someone is calling out my name. I begin to walk forward so I can hear better, and before long, I'm running so fast I can't stop. The voice is so familiar. Finally, I see where it's coming from. It's the most glorious vision I've ever seen. A crowd of people, shouting my name and cheering me on—some I recognize and some I don't—but all of them are cheering just for me. And when they see me, they cheer even louder, as if I'm about to score a winning run.

Then I see him. His face is shining, and his eyes are locked onto mine. I know him at once. He's my Creator, my Savior. He doesn't wait for me to reach him, but he runs to me and embraces me with tears flooding his face.

I'm home! I'm home. And I'm surrounded by the ones I love most—precious people who have interceded on my behalf to our Creator and with their prayers created a hedge of protection around me that nothing could penetrate.

Have you ever taken a detour on the journey of life? Have you strayed from the narrow road and been enticed by the sights and sounds of the masses? Have you lost your way and felt you could never find your way back home? We've all been there. We've all strayed. We've all wandered off the path. But your story can end just like mine. The road to your loving heavenly Father is always lit, and you are always welcome on it. There are people there who are cheering you on, even now, and there is a Savior who waits longingly for you to turn your face toward home. When you take those first steps toward home, he'll run to meet you.

It's so easy to get distracted and turn from the path God has laid out for us. And when we find ourselves in those dark places, we do things we wouldn't want anyone to see. If the light were turned on our sin, we would be horrified. If ever you find yourself doing something you wouldn't want the people you respect to know about, a loud alarm should sound in your head and warn you to stop! But God does see everything we do. Imagine living in a house of mirrors. Everywhere you look, there you are. Everything you do, you see yourself do. God is our house of mirrors. Everywhere we go, he goes. Everything we do, He sees. Everything we say, he hears.

The challenge is to remain constantly aware and mindful of his presence and to keep our feet planted firmly on his path. Because I carry the name of Christ, I am called to live by a higher standard. I will never be like him completely, but I will strive to be more like him every day.

And if I stray, he faithfully waits for me at the end of the well-lit road.

questions

1. What was the last spiritual high that you experienced? What got you to that mountaintop?
2. What was the last spiritual low you experienced? How did you end up in that valley?
3. What one thing is constant no matter where we find ourselves in our life's journey?
4. What people in your life cheer you on? Who calls your name when you stray from God's path?
5. Are you currently involved in any activity that you would not want the light of God shined on? Are you doing anything you would not want the people you respect to know about? What steps can you take to get you back on the narrow road?

. . . *Father of light,*

Help me live in such a way that I need not fear the light of discovery. Guide my feet and help me stay on the narrow road. Forgive me for the times that I turn away from your loving light and pursue the dangers of worldly pleasures. I praise you for the light of your Word and for your steadfast love.

ten

Jesus doesn't care . . . . .

If my people, who are called by my

name, will humble themselves and

pray and seek my face and turn from

their wicked ways, then will I hear

from heaven and will forgive their sin

and will heal their land.

—2 Chronicles 7:14

You'll tell me no one would love you
If they could see deep inside
You say your friends might desert you
If they knew the truth you hide,
Well there's One who knows you better
   than you know yourself
And He still loves you more than anybody
   else

(Chorus)

. . . . Jesus doesn't care . . . .

what you've done before
How you've rebelled or slammed the door
No matter how far you've run or how long
   you've been untrue
Jesus doesn't care
He still offers forgiveness to you
For so long you've run from the Father
Into a life of sin
And each time He lovingly called you
You turned your back on Him
No matter if your failures are great or
   small
There's no way to hide them
He already knows them all

(Chorus)

How many tears will you cry
Till you cry out to the Father
An honest plea for mercy He will not
   deny
Trust Him and you're gonna find

(Chorus)

. . from the album, life love & other mysteries . . .

You, my friend, are loved.

Don't be afraid that God will

give you a beating. He's not

that kind of father.

Denise Jones

. . . . . *G*uilt is one of the worst feelings. I guess that's why Satan likes to use it so much. It begins in a small drawer in a filing cabinet in the back of your mind, and it grows and eats at your soul. Oh, how you long to be forgiven, but you don't dare tell a soul because you are so filled with shame.

Almost on a daily basis, Point of Grace receives letters in which people share their grief and pain and guilt. Why do they write to us? I guess they feel safer writing to someone who doesn't really know them. Some tell of abortions, others of eating disorders. Some are victims of abuse, drugs, or alcohol. And many, many are eaten up with guilt and are desperate to find relief. We frequently read things like, "God could never forgive *me*. I can't tell anyone what I've done. No one would understand." But God *can* forgive, and he *does* understand. It is always my prayer that those who write will come to understand God's love for them.

I have known of God's love ever since I was a toddler in the nursery at church. But this past year, I saw God's love in a new way. One night, late in January, Stu and I stood outside our little bathroom, waiting on the results of a pregnancy test. It was a long three minutes. Would it be plus or minus? Finally, when the time was up, we dared to peek at the little stick. And there it was as plain as day—a pink plus sign! We stood in shock and bewilderment. Could it really be true? Two weeks later, a visit to the doctor assured us that it was. I was six weeks pregnant.

During the nine-month waiting period, as I watched my body stretch into funny shapes, I became increasingly aware of what a miracle we all are. God orchestrates every single detail of how babies grow, and he gives them everything they need to grow into complete human beings.

Then, after experiencing the birthing process—the details of which we don't need to go into—my awe for God's love grew even more. I can't understand how anyone who has experienced a birth could say there is no God. But not until I held little Spence in my arms did I begin to get an idea of how much God must love us. Stu and I gazed at Spence in amazement; we counted every finger and toe. His hands looked just like his daddy's and his mouth was just like mine.

As I gazed into his little face, I was overwhelmed with the intensity of the love I felt for him. As his mother, I would do anything to protect him—I can't imagine how I would feel if something happened to that little boy. That's when it hit me. God must have loved his own little boy even more than I love mine. Yet, he allowed his only Son to walk upon this cruel earth, knowing that he would have to suffer excruciating pain and die on a cross. God chose to do that for you and me.

And even before God formed us in his image, he knew that we would betray him and scorn his love. He knew all of this, and yet he created us and sent his Son to die for us anyway. If God did all this for us, knowing all the evil we would do, don't you think he was already prepared to forgive us? God is always ready and willing to forgive us if we just ask him.

You, my friend, are loved. Don't be afraid that God will give you a beating. He's not that kind of father. Even in my finite love for Spence, I know that if he someday does something terribly wrong, I will still love him. Yes, I would be disappointed, and the surprise of his wrong would shock me, but my love would not waver. While our sin disheartens and hurts God, it does not take him by surprise. He knows everything about us. He knows our weaknesses and our sin, yet he loves us anyway. If you are his son or daughter, nothing can or will affect his love for you.

Go ahead; take a chance. Do it today. Tell God what you've done and how you feel. He already knows, but he wants you to allow him to forgive and restore your precious soul.

questions

1. What was the last thing that made you feel guilty? Have you confessed that sin to God and found relief?
2. If you could write to someone you didn't know and tell them your darkest secret, knowing that this person would never tell anyone and you would never be embarrassed by seeing that person, what would you write?
3. Do you have trouble believing that God could forgive you for your darkest sins? If so, why?
4. How does the fact that God already knows everything about you make it easier for you to confess your sin to him?

. . . *Father of forgiveness,*

I bring to you the secret sins that eat me up with guilt. I am afraid and unsure, but I'm taking a chance and I'm bringing them to you. Please forgive me for the wrong I've done. I'm so sorry for causing you such pain. Thank you so much for providing the perfect sacrifice for my sin in your Son, Jesus. I praise you for your sacrifice of love and ask that you heal my soul.

eleven

saving grace . . . . . .

The entire law is

summed up in a

single command:

"Love your neighbor

as yourself."

—Galatians 5:14

She had her father's blue eyes
He left home before she arrived
Mama named her Grace
Just getting by on their own
When Grace was fifteen she ran from
   home
One December day
Grace is lost and alone in a world as cold
   as stone
God is counting on us to reach her with
   His love

(Chorus)
It's all about saving grace
All about living love
Being Jesus to those He came to save
Sharing life and giving our own away
It's all about serving God
All about . . .

. . . . *saving grace* . . . .

She'd never darken the door of any church
She would say, "What for . . . no one there
   would care for me"
We have to go where she lives
Simply show her who Jesus is
Watch Him set her free
For grace flows down from above and faith
   requires a selfless love
For a world that's dying to see the hope in
   you in me

(Chorus)

(Bridge)
There are countless millions just like
  Grace
Who need a merciful embrace
They won't believe our God is real
Until they feel His touch

(Chorus)

. . . *from the album, steady on* . . . .

As you share God's grace

• •

through a life lived in love . . .

you become *his* hands,

his feet,

his voice.

Shelley Breen

*i*t's all about saving grace;
It's all about living love.

Life is about all sorts of things, but mostly, it's about living love. Now, I know that's easy to say, but what does "living love" really mean? I believe it means pressing toward the goal of being a loving person to everyone, at all times, in any situation. It is improbable that any person, except Jesus, could actually live up to this goal. Yet, isn't loving others the second most important commandment? Jesus said the command to "love your neighbor as yourself" is second only to the command to love God (see Matt. 22:39 and Mark 12:31). The apostle Paul, in the book of Philippians, gets down to telling us *how* to love others: "Do nothing out of selfish ambition or vain conceit, but in humility consider others better than yourselves" (Phil. 2:3). Ouch! Do *nothing* out of selfish ambition? Consider others *better* than myself? Those are tall orders, but this is what we are called to do.

Being on the road provides special challenges to love others; but in reality, my challenges are probably much the same as yours. Sometimes, I'm just "too busy," "too tired," or too "turned off" to show love to the people God places in front of me. One of my all-time favorite lyrics is from a song by Scott Krippayne called "I Will Love." To me, it says it all: "I will love, for to follow Christ is to lay aside my right to choose who I will love." When we make a decision to follow Christ, we don't get to choose whom we will love. As followers of him, we give up that choice. We are called to love our enemies, beggars, the homeless—people whom the world considers unlovely and unlovable. These are the people most in need of our love, but too often, these are the people we withhold our love from. We are uncomfortable reaching out to the outcasts of society. But Jesus wasn't uncomfortable with it. In fact, he spent a large portion of his time with the most sinful people in the community. And he calls us to do the same.

I'm so thankful for the people at Mercy Ministries who reach out to girls like Grace—girls who have messed up, run away, and been in situations that have broken them down so much that they feel unlovable and alone. We are quick to judge people who look different, smell different, act different, or come from a different background. When God places a person in your life who is difficult to love, try to remember that you don't know where he or she has come from or what difficulties brought that person to the current situation.

Mercy Ministries can remind us all of the value of reaching out to those whom society shuns—pregnant teenagers, kids on drugs, teens living on the streets. As you share God's grace through a life lived in love, you become an instrument of God—you become his hands, his feet, his voice—to people desperately in need of love.

It's all about saving grace. It's all about getting our hands dirty helping the hurting, so they can see that Christ has saving grace and love for them. They'll never believe us—not for a minute—if we don't reach out and love them exactly as they are.

Just the other day, I heard a preacher say, "When it's all said and done, there are only two kinds of people in the world—saved and unsaved." It's my hope that we can live love in a way that demonstrates God's saving grace to lost and hurting souls.

questions

1. Who do you know who most demonstrates saving grace? What is it about this person that speaks God's grace?
2. What part of your life especially needs to feel God's grace?
3. Is there someone in your life whom you have chosen not to love? Will you begin to love that person today?
4. Who do you know who is not a Christian who needs to hear the message of God's saving grace?

. . . . *God of grace,*

Father of mercy, you are all that I need. How can I say thank you for the saving grace you have offered me through the death of your Son. That you would pay such a price for my soul fills me with awe. Thank you. Help me to see others through eyes of grace. Soften my heart to those who are unloved and in need. Give me opportunities to be a vessel of your grace to others and help me not to miss or ignore the opportunities you send my way. I praise you and exalt your name, O God of grace.

twelve

keep the candle burning . . .

God is our refuge

and strength, a

very present

help in trouble.

—Psalm 46:1 NRSV

You think you're alone there in your silent
  storm but I've seen the tears you've
  cried
Falling down and trying to drown
The flame of hope inside
Let me tell you now, tell you now

(Chorus)
When you're walking in the dead of night
When your soul is churning
When your hope seems out of sight
Keep the candle burning
All it takes is one steady heart in a world
  that's turning
Shine a light and pierce the dark
Keep the candle burning

. . . keep the candle burning . . .

When you're down and you're discouraged
When the darkness clouds your view
You've got to gather up your courage
You know the Lord is gonna see you
  through
Let me tell you now
Tell you now

(Chorus)

One ray of light always breaks
  through
Follow wherever He takes you
Wherever He takes you

(Chorus)

. . from the album, life love & other mysteries . . .

We all long to know

that someone sees our

tears and cares.

Terry Jones

. . . . $\mathcal{H}$ave you ever felt lonely? I know I have. I think all of us feel lonely from time to time. We feel as if no one cares whether we're here or not here, as if we are a nonentity . . . as if our life doesn't matter . . . as if no one understands.

For me, the worst loneliness is in a room full of people or when you're with a group of people but aren't really a part. Junior high and high school were the height of loneliness for me. But I also remember times in college when I felt lonely and all alone. I feel it now sometimes too.

Some people feel lonely because they're single and don't see any prospect of a mate, and some are lonely because they don't have a close family. I think many of us would be surprised to find out that people of great notoriety or popularity often feel lonely too.

I've been reading *Character Is the Issue* by Mike Huckabee, who is currently the governor of Arkansas. He is a devout Christian and a wonderful man. We've had the privilege of meeting with him on a few occasions and have visited the governor's mansion. In reading this book, what has struck me most about the governor is not his views on governing or how he proposes to solve today's problems but the deep sense of loneliness he so often feels. He is a well-loved man, but it is obvious in his writing that he often feels a sense of abandonment, even by his closest friends. Any time you stand up for what is right, some people will criticize your successes. Barbara Johnson calls them "joy robbers"—people who suck all the joy out of your moment of victory. Mike Huckabee experiences this constantly.

Sometimes you can hear a million comments on how well you've handled something or what a great job you've done, but if one person says something negative, that negative comment is all you'll remember. That happens a lot with our ministry. We can get a hundred positive comments and only one negative, but that one negative really stings and seems to overshadow all the good. Today, when I get discouraged, I try to look at the positive things in my life. I call on God to remind me of the good going on around me and that he is with me in my loneliness.

Point of Grace has received lots of letters over the years about the songs we sing, but the song that continues to get the most response is "Jesus Will Still Be There." I think the reason it touches so many people is that we all want to know that there is someone we can count on. We want to be secure in the knowledge that we are deeply loved and that God will see us through. Praise God that the message of this song is true! We *can* count on him, we *are* deeply loved, and he will *always* see us through!

The line that touches me most in "Keep the Candle Burning" is the first one: "You think you're alone there in your silent storm, but I've seen the tears you've cried." Isn't that what we all long for, to know that someone sees our tears and cares? But when we are desperate and in pain, we lose all perspective and we forget that God is there. At times like this, we need to stop for just a minute, refocus, and remember that God really is there. We need to be still in the knowledge that he is God; we need to calmly rest in the safety of his hands. And if we can remember to do this, then, when we look up again, the sky will seem a little brighter and we'll be able to see the end of the tunnel.

I see the storms of life like tornados. Just last week, we witnessed the destruction of homes and office buildings when a tornado tore through Nashville. The videos of the tornado show that when you see it from far off, you can see the shape of the funnel cloud and the path it is taking. But as the tornado gets closer, things become less clear, and all of a sudden you have no perspective at all because you are right in the middle of the storm. The tornado twists and turns, and you can't find a way out. Then when it's over, you can see the sky again.

That's what losing your focus is like. Everything around you blurs, but if you can keep from panicking, take a deep breath, and remember that God is there, you will survive the storm with much less trauma. And soon, you will be able to see the sky again.

I want to be a gentle reminder for all of us who think we are alone in our silent storms. I want to remind us that God can and will protect us. We just have to let him. God promises to protect those who love him: "Because he loves me," says the Lord, "I will rescue him; I will protect him, for he acknowledges my name. He will call upon me, and I will answer him; I will be with him in trouble, I will deliver him and honor him" (Ps. 91:14–15).

So, today, if there is a big or small storm in your life, sit back and call his name and ask him to give you perspective. Ask him to rescue you and deliver you from trouble. His rescue does not always come in the form of taking away the pain or magically making everything better, but his rescue always brings peace and a sense of security and the knowledge that Someone cares. You don't have to feel alone. Just hang in there, try not to freak out, and keep your candle burning steady. The tornado may pick you up, but it will always set you back down again.

It is how we choose to live that gives us perspective on what is around us. Make the choice to rest in him.

questions

1. When was the last time you felt really lonely? What caused you to feel lonely?
2. How can focusing on God help you feel less lonely?
3. Have you ever felt the confusion and turmoil of a "tornado" as described in the devotional? Were you able to call for God in the tornado, or did you feel so confused that you forgot?
4. If you called for God in your last "tornado," how did he help?

. . . . God of refuge,

Thank you that you come to my rescue when my life becomes a tornado. The next time I face a tornado, help me remember to call on you. Please give me the perspective I need to survive the storm and even to grow and learn from it. Bring me to the point of maturity that I can even thank you for the storms, knowing that learning to handle storms with grace can make me more like you.

thirteen

God forbid . . . . . .

Be still,

and know that

I am God.

—Psalm 46:10

The more I know Your power, Lord
The more I'm mindful
How casually we speak and sing Your
    name
How often we have come to You
With no fear or wonder
And called upon You only for what we
    stand to gain

(Chorus)
God forbid, that I find You so familiar
That I think of You as less than who
    You are
God forbid, that I should speak of You
    at all
Without a humble reverence in my heart

. . . . God forbid . . . .

Lord, I often talk about Your love and
    mercy
How it seems to me Your goodness has
    no end
It frightens me to think that I could take
    You for granted
Though You're closer than a brother
You're more than just my friend

(Chorus)

You are my Father, God Almighty
Lord of Lords, You're King of Kings
Beyond my understanding
No less than everything

(Chorus)

God forbid
God forbid

. . . from the album, life love & other mysteries . . .

The gentle breeze

turned into a wind of

mercy and grace,

blowing all that finally

· ·

confessed sin out of

me, leaving me

cleaned and renewed.

Heather Floyd

.... *L*ast summer, I was driving along the California coastline, near beautiful Monterey. I was on a mission. We were singing in the area, and we had the day off, so I had decided to dedicate this day to spending time with God. No distractions, no tasks to complete, just God and me.

I'd started my day with an early breakfast at a quaint little sidewalk café in Monterey. When I left the café the sun was shining through a thin layer of clouds. As I drove along the coast, the sun danced on the water. In a word, it was breathtaking! I soon found a beautiful little spot, pulled over, and stopped the car. I thanked the Lord for his creation and for making it so obvious that his hand had orchestrated it all. I thanked him for perfecting all my imperfections and for giving us moments like these for soaking it all in.

I started the car again and continued my journey along the cliffs. Just as I passed a lighthouse, I found what I didn't know I had been looking for. It was a special meeting place for just God and me. Right in the middle of the hillside, about five hundred feet above the Pacific Ocean was a big rock. I don't know why I was drawn to this particular place, but I desperately wanted to get to that rock. So I got my Bible, a bottle of water, and my journal and headed for my rock. I trudged through stickers, weeds, and thorny bushes that scraped up my legs, but I didn't care; I was on an adventure. I was making my way to this rock, and nothing was going to stop me.

Finally, I made it, only to discover that if, before I began my trek up the mountain, I had walked a few steps farther, I would have come to a clear path right to the rock. Oh well, my way had been much more interesting.

At first, I just sat on the rock and looked out at the vast ocean below me. I felt so free, sitting so high above everything. It was like God was saying, "Heather, be still and know that I am God. Don't question or overspiritualize; don't talk; just know that I am God." I closed my eyes and felt a gentle breeze blowing through my hair. Away from everything and everyone, my mind was clear.

I started remembering times when I had been disobedient and unfaithful to God. And then I remembered that every time I had wavered, his undying love had carried me through. As I continued to meditate, I was reminded of the promises from his Word that he does not even remember our sin. In the book of Jeremiah he declares, "I will forgive their wickedness and will remember their sins no more" (Jer. 31:34). And in Psalm 103:12, we read, "As far as the east is from the west, so far has he removed our transgressions from us." The gentle breeze turned into a wind of mercy and grace, blowing all that finally confessed sin out of me, leaving me clean and renewed. He opened my eyes to see, once again, how fortunate I am to be able to come boldly before his throne of grace.

Savoring this holy moment, I was reminded of the story in Matthew 7 about the wise man who built his house upon the rock. Every kind of imaginable storm descended on the house, and still it stood because it was firmly secured on the rock. There have been numerous times in my life when I either lived in fear of losing everything or when everything really did seem to fall apart. However, if we've chosen to build on the solid rock, just like the house in Jesus' parable, we will stand. Even if everything around us is crumbling, our feet will remain firmly planted on the rock, and we will stand on solid ground. The ground beneath our feet may be all that's intact, but it will be enough, and it will remain steadfast throughout the storm.

God is my rock, my redeemer, my refuge in troubled times. He is my strength, my deliverer, my judge, my companion. He is everything I need. Sometimes we get so involved in this world that we forget what we have in God. As the song "God Forbid" says,

> The more I know Your power, Lord
> The more I'm mindful
> How often we have come to You
> With no fear or wonder
> And called upon You only for what we stand to
> gain

God forbid that we should take him for granted. I learned a lot sitting on my rock, high above the ocean. I found there a refuge from the rest of the world; I was forced, in a good way, to a place of surrender and abandonment. Spending time alone with God is absolutely essential. It is there alone with him that we are able to focus on the unseen and the eternal. He wants to share things about himself with us, but we must be still and quiet in order to hear.

My story doesn't end there. When I got back to Nashville, my legs started itching, and little blisters began to form. I went to the emergency room to discover that I had poison sumac, which is common to that part of California. Those itching blisters turned out to be a gentle reminder of the precious time I had spent alone with God on my rock. It was an experience I'll never forget!

questions

1. When did you last spend some time alone with God? What did you talk about? How did he bless you?
2. Why is it so important to spend quiet time alone with God? Why don't we get the same benefit in a group or in a noisy, busy place?
3. Why is it important to build your house on the Rock, now, before the storms come? Why not just try to make your way to the Rock after the storm hits?
4. Do you ever take God for granted? What helps you to be more aware of his wonder and awe?

. . . . *awesome Father,*

Forgive me when I take you for granted. Fill my heart with awe and respect for you. Thank you that even though you are so powerful, you allow me to come boldly before your throne of grace anytime I want to. Deepen my heart so that I can hold more of you in me. Enrich my spirit so that I can develop a more intimate relationship with you.

fourteen

better days . . . .

And after you suffer for a short time,

God, who gives all grace, will make

everything right. He will make you strong

and support you and keep you from falling.

He called you to share in his glory in Christ,

a glory that will continue forever.

—1 Peter 5:10 NCV

It's a heart attack a minute
In this life down here on earth
We're all stranded right here in it
Wondering what it's worth
There are always threads of trouble
In this tangled web we weave
But tomorrow may just be OK
See here's what I believe

(Chorus)
Better days are on the way my friend
Just a ways on down the line
I believe that just around the bend
Everything's gonna be fine
Better days are just a dream right now
It's like all you do is pray
But the world keeps turning
Bringing us

better days . . . .

Well the storms won't stop descending
And the rain won't cease to fall
And there ain't no use pretending
'Cause it's bound to find us all
Well it's easy to get hopeless
And drive yourself insane
But before you stop and set up shop
In the middle of the pain
(Remember)

(Chorus)

(Bridge)
I know you've heard all the platitudes
About attitudes and positive thinking
But time just keeps marching on
So just hold on
This too will pass
I know you'll see your face in a smile
   again

(Chorus)

(Chorus)

I believe in better days

. . . *from the album, steady on* . . . .

BETTER DAYS. Words and music by Regie Hamm ©1998
McSpadden Smith Music/Yolanda's Fine Music/ SESAC

Everything around you

may be falling apart. . . .

But, my friend,

what happened

at the Cross

declares victory

to all believers.

Denise Jones

. . . . *L*ife is hard, isn't it? We all have had our share of disappointment, pain, and grief. As I sit here watching the ten o'clock news, the hopeless state of our world is plain to see. It's depressing to see all the pain and destruction around us. Some things we bring on ourselves, but others, such as tornadoes, floods, or car accidents, are completely outside our control.

Some of you reading this are going through intense pain right now. Perhaps you've lost someone you love to death or to the world. Maybe your relationship with your most important person in the world is falling apart. Maybe your health or physical disabilities keep you from living life as you'd like. My heart is heavy for those of you who hurt.

The book of 1 Peter (5:8) tells us that the devil (our enemy) goes around like a roaring lion looking for someone to eat. You and I both know he doesn't want us to succeed. I don't know why we are so surprised on those days when absolutely nothing goes right. What do we expect? We live in a world ruled by the Prince of Darkness. Peter confirms this: "Dear friends, do not be surprised at the painful trial you are suffering, as though something strange were happening to you" (1 Pet. 4:12). We are told over and over that we will go through suffering.

But I don't really want to talk about suffering. We're all familiar with it, on some level. What I want to talk about is *hope*. What do you hope for? I hope I'll stay healthy. I hope Point of Grace will continue to do well. I hope that tomorrow is sunny. I hope a lot of things. But I don't think this is the kind of hope Christ tells us about. One definition of hope is "to anticipate with pleasure; waiting with expectancy." In the New Testament, hope centers on Jesus Christ himself. He is our hope.

My mom and I were talking on the phone the other day. She had experienced a horrible day, and it wasn't getting any better. As we continued to talk, the Holy Spirit began to remind us of scriptures of promise, and we shared what he brought to our mind:

> Peace I leave with you; my peace I give you.
> (John 14:27)

I have told you these things, so that in me you may have peace. In this world you will have trouble. But take heart! I have overcome the world. (John 16:33)

"For I know the plans I have for you," declares the Lord, "plans to prosper you and not to harm you, plans to give you hope and a future." (Jer. 29:11)

Hope and a future! Isn't that what we all want? God has plans for us—plans to prosper us. Isn't that wonderful? How blessed we are!

Have you ever watched a rerun of a ball game when you already knew the outcome, and you knew your team had won? The others watching the game who don't know the outcome are going completely bonkers! They're screaming and yelling and are all worked up. You, on the other hand, are calm and collected. Your team may fall apart and have a bad quarter, but you know that eventually, things are going to turn around. You may get a little nervous watching the bad parts, but you are calmed by the expectant hope and knowledge that your team is going to win.

The same principle applies to the Christian walk. We know how the game turns out. The message of the Bible is that we win! Everything around you may be falling apart. You may lose your cool and get angry with a coworker or family member; you may get so depressed you don't know how you will go on. But, my friend, what happened at the Cross declares victory to all believers. The prince of this world is powerless in light of his love.

I don't know all the answers to why we have to suffer in this life, but I do know that if it never rained, we wouldn't know how to appreciate the beautiful sunshine. If we never experienced pain, we wouldn't know the joy of relief. Though we can't answer all the *whys*, we can know that his grace in our lives will make everything right.

No matter how dreary things may look in the third quarter, our God will work everything together for good. Even if in this life we don't see the physical victory, we remain confident that better days are ahead, for our hope is not based on what we can see, but on the unseen. "For in this hope we were saved. But hope that is seen is no hope at all. Who hopes for what he already has? But if we hope for what we do not yet have, we wait for it patiently" (Rom. 8:24–25).

Better days are on the way. Hold on, sometimes it just takes time. Know that your hope in Jesus will make you strong and keep you from falling. Remember the words of this old song: "My hope is built on nothing less than Jesus' blood and righteousness."

questions

1. How can hope in a future heaven help you get through your current pain?
2. What evidence do you see in your life of God's plan to "prosper you" and "give you hope and a future"?
3. Have you already been through a storm in your life and made it through to better days? What does that teach you about future storms?
4. How does the hope of Christ make it easier for Christians to weather storms than non-Christians?

. . . . *God of future hope,*

Hold me steady while I wait for better days. Help me keep my spiritual eyes focused on the unseen hope and not get depressed by looking at the seen despair. Forgive me when I doubt your love for me and your desire and ability to bring me through. I praise you for your promises to give me better days.

fifteen

this day . . . .

He died for us so that, whether we

are awake or asleep, we may live

together with him. Therefore

encourage one another and build

each other up, just as

. . . you are doing.

—1 Thessalonians 5:10–11

This day is fragile
Soon it will end
And once it has vanished, it will not come
  again
So let us love with a love pure and strong
Before this day is gone

This day is fleeting
When it slips away
Not all our money can buy back this day
So let us pray that we might be a friend
Before this day is spent

This day we're given is golden
Let us show love

. . . . *this day* . . . .

  is ours for one moment
Let us sow love

This day is frail. It will pass by
So, before it's too late to recapture
  the time
Let us share love. Let us share God
Before this day is gone
Before this day is gone

. . . from the album, point of grace . . . .

N

Nothing

can bring

back God's

gift of today.

Shelley Breen

. . . . *O*n the last day of Grandpa's life, he was very still and quiet. As I sat holding his hand, I wondered about his future.

I still remember my mom calling me at college to tell me that Grandpa had cancer and that it was bad. Over the next few months, his cancer spread rapidly throughout his body, and it became obvious that death was inevitable. Although Papa had a hard time expressing his love outwardly, all his children and grandchildren knew that he loved them very much. And even though he and I weren't especially close, he was very dear to me. His whole life, Grandpa had been a good, honest, hard-working man. While his exterior was somewhat stern, his heart was gentle and kind.

I have to be honest with you and tell you that until Grandpa got sick, I'd never thought about whether or not he believed in Jesus. But as his death grew closer, I began to feel a desperate need to talk with him about his salvation and where he would be spending eternity. But I couldn't get up the nerve to approach the subject. And as his body and mind deteriorated, I was afraid of offending him or reminding him that his days were numbered.

And so, on the last day of his life, as I sat with my grandpa, holding his hand, my heart was heavy and burdened. He said nothing, but for one brief moment he squeezed my hand to acknowlege my presence. A few hours later, he passed away.

During the next few days before the funeral, I worried and wondered where my grandfather was spending his eternity. Though I told no one, I felt guilty, selfish, and stupid that I had not been able to swallow my pride and talk with Papa about Jesus while he was still alive. I came up with a million reasons why I hadn't, but not a single one was reason enough—not when it had been a matter of eternal life and death.

But on the day of the funeral, the preacher said something that filled me with joy. As he spoke to the gathered crowd, he told us that a few weeks before his death, Papa had telephoned him and asked him to come visit him. My grandfather told that sweet preacher that he wanted to spend eternity with Jesus. They prayed together, and Papa accepted Christ. As the preacher finished the story, I cried tears of relief—but also tears of shame. I was ashamed that it was a preacher instead of me who shared words of eternal significance with my grandfather. I who sang Christian music, I who was his own flesh and blood, I had been afraid to open my mouth and say the words.

After the service, I found the preacher in the parking lot and hugged his neck. "Thank you for telling my Papa about Jesus!" I'm still thankful to him today.

As the song says,

> This day is frail. It will pass by
> So, before it's too late to recapture the time
> Let us share love. Let us share God
> Before this day is gone

Although I did share love with my grandpa, I didn't share God.

Is there someone in your life you need to share Christ with? I urge you not to be like me and leave it to someone else. Today is the day of salvation, not tomorrow. Nothing can bring back God's gift of today. Open your mouth and share the Good News before it is too late.

questions

1. Who do you know who needs to hear about Jesus?
2. What things keep you from sharing Jesus with people you love?
3. How has knowing Jesus changed you life? Choose one positive change he's brought into your life; think of a way to share it in conversation.

. . . . . .  *Father,*

It is so easy to remain silent when I should be sharing the Good News of Jesus. It is so tempting to allow pride or fear to overcome the urgency to speak to those who have never been born again. I don't mean to fail you or those I love. Please forgive me when I allow opportunities to slip away without a word of truth or salvation being uttered from these lips you have made clean. Give me the courage to be as bold and as loving as my Savior and to say the most important words anyone could ever hear—Jesus saves.

living the legacy . . . . .

He . . . established the law in Israel,

which he commanded our forefathers

to teach their children, so the next

generation would know them, even

the children yet to be born, and they

in turn would tell their children.

—Psalm 78:5–6

My father knew it
And his before him
And it goes way back down the line
They had a vision
A prayer for the future
For what I would believe in time
Now I'm not perfect
Life's not easy
But I wouldn't take the world for what they
gave to me

(Chorus)
I'm living the legacy
Walking the path that the faithful have laid
down
I'm . . .

. . . . . *living the legacy* . . . . .

Finding the hope that my fathers found
I am standing tall when I'm on my knees
I'm living the legacy

Something in common
Deep inside me
With those before me who are gone
Gives me the vision
Fills me with a passion
To make the message carry on

144

Now I'm not perfect
Life's not easy
But for the future's sake I'm gonna
   do the best I can

(Chorus 3x)

. . . *from the album, point of grace* . . . .

LIVING THE LEGACY. Words and music by Geoff Thurman & Lowell Alexander ©1993 P.E. Velvet Music (a div.
of the Harding Music Group)/Seventh Son Music (a div.
of the Glen Campbell Music Group)/Birdwing Music (a
div. of the Sparrow Corp.) Adm. by BMG Songs,
Inc./BMG Songs, Inc. (Gospel Div.) (ASCAP)

We don't have to be perfect,

thank goodness.

We just have to try

to do the best we can.

Terry Jones

family devotionals were a ritual in our family. Every morning before school, Mom wakened my three sisters and me at 6:30. At that hour of the morning, we didn't feel at all spiritual and we certainly didn't want to get out of bed. Sometimes we had to do a couple of minutes of aerobics before reading the Bible just to stay awake. Nonetheless, Mom and Dad consistently woke us up and insisted that we start the day off right. They had a vision for the future that we couldn't see.

They were passing on the legacy of faith they had learned from the generation before them. My grandparents on both sides are deeply committed to God. One of the most precious legacies they are passing on to me is the legacy of lifelong marriages. As I write this, my heart is filled with a heavy sadness because my sweet grandmother passed away last Monday. Her death stirred memories of childhood and the legacy of faith she passed on to me and all her other grandchildren. Gram had such a brilliant mind and an avid interest in culture and history, and she passed those interests on to me as part of her legacy. But more than that, she gave me a legacy of faith. Even as a child, I could see the strength of her faith and the firmness of her conviction.

I am thankful for the legacy of faith I see in all my precious grandparents. And I am thankful that they passed that faith on to my parents, who lived it before my sisters and me every day of our lives. My dad's favorite song is "Living the Legacy." And now, the legacy of faith has become a part of me. I feel so blessed to be a descendant of godly men and women who taught their children and their children's children to know God.

I don't remember many details from those early morning devotionals all those years ago. I couldn't tell you the topics in the devotional book we used or which Bible verses we read, but I do remember the principles of discipline and commitment and the value of studying God's Word.

Now that I am a new mom, I want to pass this godly legacy on to our precious son, Cole. Even though we've only had our little guy for seven weeks, already I know I would give my life for him. I have so many questions about how to care for this new baby, and sometimes it's hard to believe that Chris and I are raising a child. But when I sit back and think, I realize that it all comes down to love and commitment. And when I look into the sparkling eyes of my beautiful baby and see how his face lights up when he hears my voice, my heart is filled to overflowing with love and I know that I can give him all the love he needs. When I remember the daily devotionals from my childhood, I realize that the legacy of faith is lived out *one day at a time,* and I think that I can do the same. Because my parents instilled Christlike qualities in our lives through their love and commitment, the legacy of their faith has been passed on to another generation.

As the song says,

> I'm not perfect, life's not easy,
> But for the future's sake,
> I'm gonna do the best I can.

To me that means that while we all are bound to make lots of mistakes, we have a lot more at stake than just today. We don't have to be perfect, thank goodness. We just have to try to do the best we can. I think I can handle trying. We are all building generations to come, and we can do it with God's guidance and wisdom—one day at a time with love and devotion to him.

I realize that some of you reading this may not have a Christian heritage. But the legacy can begin with you. Christ, our big brother, makes all things new, and God, our heavenly Father, passes on his legacy of hope so that you can live his legacy and "make the message carry on."

questions

1. What rituals from your childhood are now a part of you that you want to pass on to your children?
2. Who in your past helped shape you spiritually?
3. Who are you shaping spiritually right now?
4. How can you build on the legacy you received from your past to leave an even better one for your children?

Father of past and present,

Thank you for the people you've put in my life who have shaped me for eternity. Give me vision to see the value of the legacy I've received from past generations. Help me live my life with an awareness of my impact on the future. Forgive me for the times when I've selfishly lived for the moment, disregarding the eternal consequences. Thank you for the inheritance you have laid up for me in Jesus Christ. Teach me to appreciate its value and to share it with others.

seventeen

you are the answer . . . . .

I am the way and

the truth and the

life. No one

comes to the

Father except

through me.

—John 14:6

They line the Wailing Wall
The masses fill up St. Peter's Square
Confessions, emotions
Spill out of desperate prayer
I know they're not alone
They've come to face the penitence stone
I hear the voices, the souls in need of
  You, 'cause

(Chorus)
You are the answer
And the meaning of life
To hearts in darkness
You're the source of light
As we walk this human road
Every question will find

. . . . . you are the answer . . . .

Across the playground yard
Another future society
Living and learning
The way it's supposed to be
The days of truth grow dim
Your hand must reach down and write
  in them
The message of hope that can only be
  found in You, 'cause

(Chorus)

You shined Your light in me
When I had no way
Rescued my dying heart
That I could not save
And not just for me but for the world
   today

(Chorus)

. . . *from the album, life love & other mysteries* . . . .

We are "God with skin on"
to searching people.

Heather Floyd

*W*hat in the world is going on? I think what I really mean to say is what is going on in the world? It seems as if every time I turn on CNN, I hear something truly devastating. Children killing children, people building bombs that kill thousands of innocent people, even a human being trying to create a virus that could infect and kill an entire nation, if not the whole world. What is this all about? Why would someone want to destroy life? What makes a mind desire evil?

I know these are extreme cases, but destruction goes on all around us everyday. Consider the lives of people you know who don't know Christ. I know this is a heavy subject, but I feel an enormous burden to remind us all, myself include, that it's up to us to share the message that Jesus is the answer.

People everywhere are searching for solid answers to big questions. Most of them don't know it, but what they are searching for is a life-changing relationship with Almighty God. They don't know it, but they long to feel his loving grace. But in order for them to know his grace, someone must show them God's love in tangible form here on earth. We are "God with skin on" to searching people.

If you've seen the movie or the play *Les Miserables*, you've seen a beautiful story of God's love lived out in real life. Because an old bishop showed mercy to the undeserving convict, Jean Valjean, his whole life was changed, and the convict became a vessel of God's mercy and love to all who came in contact with him. We, too, know God's love. We, too, can be vessels of mercy.

But to be perfectly honest, there are times when I see all the digression in the world and find myself thinking, "It's not my fault, there's nothing I can do." *Wrong!* The message of Christ is not just for me; it's for me to share with my little corner of the world. My ministry with Point of Grace is not enough; answering fan mail is not enough; living a good Christian life is not enough; going to church is not enough. All those things are important, but they are not enough. I have to be mindful that every person I come in contact with each day needs God's wonderful grace— whether they know it or not. Jesus is the answer to all our needs. He's the answer for me. He's the answer for my pastor. He's the answer for the mailman, the plumber, the mechanic, and even the person who pulls out in front of me on the interstate. Jesus is the answer.

A long time ago, I made a mistake, and even though I made amends, I still regret to this day. I was in the tenth grade, and our youth group was having a contest for High Attendance Sunday. The Sunday school class that had the highest attendance, including visitors, would win a prize. I think it was a pizza party. Well, I was hot on the trail of prospective visitors. Who could I invite to come to church with me? I ended up inviting two of my good friends who didn't go to church anywhere, and they both agreed to come. I was so excited because now my class had a good chance of winning that contest. High Attendance Sunday came, and I picked my friends up and brought them to church. After I introduced my guests, I sat them in the corner and joined the other members of my class so we could get down to the reason we were there—counting! I just knew we were going to win. I was so excited. Eventually, I glanced over at my two friends sitting alone in the corner, and my heart felt a little pang of regret. There they sat, all alone, silently watching us salivate at the prospect of winning a pizza party. This was what they were going to think church was all about. Instead of witnessing the sweetness of God's love in action, they witnessed a group of kids concerned about one thing and one thing only—numbers! I missed a great opportunity to share Jesus with my friends. The sad fact is that I should have invited them long before High Attendance Sunday—not to win a contest, but because I cared enough for them that I wanted them to experience God's love.

Yes, I was ashamed. Yes, I asked for forgiveness, though not until years later. Most important, I learned a lesson. It's not about numbers and it never will be. It's about a world full of eternal souls longing for hope, looking for light, and searching desperately for the truth. Life is not a contest. As soldiers in God's army, we don't have time to compete with each other. We have been commissioned to be Jesus to the people we run into every day. Give grace. Reach out. Shed light. Love like God loves. Share the truth that Jesus is the answer.

questions

1. Who do you know who is searching for answers to big questions?
2. What does it mean to be "God with skin on"?
3. Have you ever found yourself caught up in something as unimportant as "numbers" while overlooking the genuine needs of people? What lessons did you learn from the experience?
4. What questions can you think of that Jesus is the answer to?

. . . . . *God of truth,*

Father of answers, please open my eyes to the questioning souls around me. Fill my heart with compassion for them, and give me the words to speak of you. Forgive me for the many times I've been so consumed with my own petty interests that I've been oblivious to the deep needs of those around me. I praise you for being the answer to all our questions.

eighteen

circle of friends . . . . .

I pray also for those who will believe

in me through their message, that all

of them may be one, Father, just as

you are in me and I am in you. May

they also be in us so that the world

may believe that you have sent me.

—John 17:20–21

We were made to love and be loved
But the price this world demands will cost
    you far too much
I spent so many lonely years just trying to
    fit in
Now I've found a place in this circle of
    friends
In a circle of friends we have one Father
In a circle of friends we share this prayer
That every orphaned soul will know
And all will enter in
To the shelter of this circle of friends

If you weep, I will weep with you
If you sing for joy the rest of us will lift our
    voices too
But no matter what you feel inside there's
    no need to pretend
That's the way it is in this circle of friends
In a . . .

. . . . *circle of friends* . . . . . .

We have one Father
In a circle of friends we share this prayer
That we'll gather together no matter how
    the highway bends
I will not lose this circle of friends
Among the nations, tribes and tongues we
    have sisters and brothers
And when we meet in heaven we will
    recognize each other
With joy so deep and love so sweet

Oh, we'll celebrate these friends
And a life that never ends
In a prayer
That will not be long before
All will enter in
To the shelter of this circle of friends
That it will not be long before
All will enter in
To the shelter of this circle of friends

. . . from the album, life love & other mysteries . .

CIRCLE OF FRIENDS. Words and music by Douglas
McKelvey and Steve Siler ©1996 River Oaks Music Co.
(adm. by EMI Christian Music Pub.)/Alright Bug Music
(adm. by EMI Christian Music Pub.)/BMI/Magnolia Hill
Music LLC (a subsidiary of McSpadden-Smith
Music)/ASCAP

point of grace life love & other mysteries

When our relationships

· ·

with our brothers and

sisters are not right,

the power of our

testimony for Christ

shrivels.

Denise Jones

. . . . . *i* believe that friendship is one of the most precious gifts God has given us here on earth. We all
want and need friends. Friends make us feel a part
of something special. Friends make us feel loved
and accepted. I can't tell you what a blessing it is to
travel with my dear friends Shelley, Heather, and
Terry. I thank God that he has surrounded me with
such a wonderful circle of friends.

Many people ask us how four girls can travel
together for such long periods of time. They want
to know if we disagree and how we really get
along. Of course, there are times when we disagree.
What good would we be to each other if we always

thought exactly the same? We have found that the keys to maintaining healthy relationships are communication and hearts that are seeking God.

Point of Grace has made a commitment to glorify God in our relationships. Now, don't get me wrong. I'm not saying we've never had tension in our group. We've worked through many tears and hurt feelings to come to this commitment. But with give and take and lots of prayer, God continues to keep our circle of friendship together and closely tied.

In our travels across the country, we've been privileged to see the inner workings of many churches. We've been to many places where the unity of Christ is evident and the fruit of the Spirit was everywhere. It is so encouraging to see people at our concerts break through denominational walls and worship our loving Father together. But, unfortunately, we have also seen disunity and tension between people in the church, whether it be between pastor and music director or between the congregation and the staff, whatever the source, the disunity affects the whole church.

Terry, Heather, and I went to church together all the way through high school. About the time we went off to college, our church went through a split. A lot of people were extremely hurt; many are still working through the pain that break in fellowship caused. Families who had been friends for years were forced to take sides. I have to think that it must make God sad to see the body of his Son torn apart.

Jesus' beautiful prayer in John 17 is partly a prayer about friendship. He begins by praying for his dear friends, his disciples. He asks God to keep them safe, to prepare their way, and to give them power in his name. And then he turns his attention toward future believers—that's us. Stop for just a minute to think on the significance of this prayer. Two thousand years ago, Jesus prayed for you and for me. That's incredible! And do you know what he prayed for? He prayed that we would *be one.*

Our unity must be extremely important to him. He said in his prayer that our unity would prove to the world that God had sent Jesus (vv. 21, 23). What a testimony he intended our unity to be! What a responsibility we have to maintain the unity he established! Because all believers have the same Father, we should unite our hearts in him.

If you knew that you had only a few days left on this earth, how would it affect how you related to other people? Would you choose your words more carefully? Would you let petty differences slide? I believe you would.

Think of a fellow believer whom you have a hard time loving. Now think of what Jesus intends your unity with that brother or sister to accomplish. When we look at it that way, it becomes evident that it's much more important to glorify God than to make our point or win an argument. If we can value our unity above our selfish desires for things to go our way, those around us will see the testimony of our love and will come to understand how much God loves them.

denise

When our relationship with our brothers and sisters is not right, the power of our testimony for Christ shrivels. I know that maintaining unity is much easier said than done. I, myself, am extremely selfish and struggle with wanting my own way. I'm involved in a never-ending battle between my will and God's way. But I am convinced that if we set our hearts on unity, God will bless our efforts and will shower us with the blessings of a circle of faithful friends.

questions

1. Who is your best friend? Why is that friendship important to you? What helps you maintain your unity?
2. How does our unity with other believers affect the way nonbelievers see God?
3. If you knew that you had only a few days left on this earth, how would it affect how you related to other people?
4. What characteristics in you sometimes threaten to damage friendships? What can you do to grow in these areas?
5. What do you see as the keys to keeping unity in friendships?

. . . *God of relationships,*

Strip me of the selfishness that threatens to damage my relationships with other believers. Help me look to a higher cause than my own. Forgive me when I soil your reputation by behaving selfishly and unlovingly. Teach me to be longsuffering with those who are difficult to get along with. I pray that my life will be a testimony to all of your love.

nineteen

Jesus is . . . .

We are therefore Christ's

ambassadors, as though God

were making his appeal

through us. We implore you

on Christ's behalf: Be

reconciled to God.

—2 Corinthians 5:20

Speak a little softer so I can hear you
Above the noise, the noise, the noise in
  this world, yeah
You don't have to shout it for hearts to
  listen
Just be a still, small voice, and let the truth
  be heard

(Chorus)
That Jesus is, Jesus is, the way, the truth,
  He is the light
For me, for you, for the world tonight
Our hope, the meaning of this life
Jesus is,

Jesus is

Jesus is, Jesus is
Everybody's looking, but how will they
  find it
The road to happiness unless they're told
That love is the answer to the ultimate
  question
But how will they understand unless they
  know

(Chorus)

The way, the truth. He is the light
For me, for you. for the world tonight
Our hope, the meaning of this life
Jesus is, Jesus is
Jesus is, Jesus is
He is the way, the truth, the light . . .

. . . *from the album, steady on* . . . .

The God of the universe is our *Father*. Why would we turn to anyone else?

Shelley Breen

*Y*ou don't have to go far on the streets of Nashville to find a store selling crystals and rocks that supposedly give you energy and brain power, or a woman reading palms for those eager for knowledge about themselves. And if you've ever stayed up late at night and channel surfed, you've probably run across a psychic network or two. I used to laugh at those things, but now I'm beginning to realize that they are symptoms of a huge problem.

People today are searching. They are looking everywhere for the truth. They long to fill their lives with purpose and meaning. They hunger for someone who will listen and care. They want to know their future and what it holds for them. These are healthy desires and interests. What isn't so healthy is where many people seek answers. Rather than turning to God and his Word, they look to "spiritualists" and worldly idealogies.

I can't help but scratch my head and wonder if some of this rampant nonsense we see in New Age philosophies, cults, and psychics isn't brought on by us Christians. I think we have failed as a body of believers to tell people that Jesus is the answer to their deepest longings and that he holds the future they so desperately long to know. Most Christians automatically look to God for the meaning of life and assurances about our future. So why haven't we gotten the word out that what people seek can be found in Jesus?

The four of us girls have a very special friend who I'll call Mary. Mary is one of the sweetest, coolest, most complimentary people you could ever meet. We met her a long time ago when she did our hair and makeup for a photo shoot. Mary has a psychic whom she relies on for the big decisions in her life. I have to be honest and say that it's really been hard for me to know what to say to Mary when her psychic comes up in conversation. My first impulse is to say, "Mary, this is ridiculous! What in the world are you thinking? Are you crazy?" But I know this kind of reaction wouldn't be helpful. I believe that God will give me the perfect opportunity to tell her that he is the way, that he knows the way, and that he knows *her* way. For now, I try to live the life of someone who has been redeemed, and I try to be a good friend to her.

The Bible is clear in its instructions to stay away from spiritists or mediums. God wants us to seek *him* for help and guidance.

> When men tell you to consult mediums and spiritists, who whisper and mutter, should not a people inquire of their God? Why consult the dead on behalf of the living? (Isa. 8:19)

> Let no one be found among you who . . . practises divination or sorcery, interprets omens, engages in witchcraft, or casts spells, or who is a medium or spiritist or who consults the dead. Anyone who does these things is detestable to the Lord. (Deut. 18:10–12)

Looking to psychics or black magic or even horoscopes to find guidance for life is a slap in the face of God. The God of the universe is our *Father;* he has given us everything we need. Why would we turn to anyone else?

I think the reason I love the song "Jesus Is" so much is that it is pure Scripture—no fancy words or metaphors, just the basics. God's truth is simple. We just have to open our mouths and say the words: Jesus is "the way, the truth, and the life." Like the song says, the noise in this world is so loud that we've got to be a still, small voice speaking the truth boldly and in love. Until we spread the word, lost people will continue to seek answers from empty sources. We know the truth; we know the light; let's tell the world in a gentle voice that Jesus is.

questions

1. Have you ever had an experience with psychics or "mediums"? Why do you think God wants us to stay away from such people?
2. How does our not sharing Jesus encourage people to turn to psychics or crystals for answers?
3. Do you have any friends who are searching for truth but looking in all the wrong places? What can you say to them to help them consider Jesus instead?
4. Which do you think is more effective with most people—being a gentle, quiet voice for Jesus or being loud and harsh? Why?

. . . *God of all truth,*

Help me to always and only look to you for truth and guidance. Give me the wisdom, the courage, and the opportunity to speak to my friends who are searching for answers but not looking to you. Help my voice to be gentle and quiet yet full of boldness and truth. Help me live my life in such a way that it too says that *Jesus is*. I praise you for being the kind of God who welcomes my questions and graciously provides guidance.

twenty

no more pain . . . .

He will wipe every tear

from their eyes. There will

be no more death or

mourning or crying or pain,

for the old order of things

has passed away.

—Revelation 21:4

She sits by the window with wandering
  eyes
She has a song in her heart and a golden
  disguise
Her body is torn because age doesn't heal
She's not letting on about the pain that she
  feels
But she knows in her soul that it won't be
  too long
'Til Jesus comes back to carry her
  home . . .

(Chorus)
Where there will be no more pain
No more sorrow
No more waiting
For illusive tomorrows
There will be . . .

. . . . *no more pain* . . . .

No more dying
No more striving or strain
No more pain
My mind's eye remembers the trouble
  I've seen
All I have been through, and how I long
  to be free
But I learn by her patience that I need her
  resolve
To wait for the opening of eternity's halls

And I know that in time we will stand
   side by side
When Jesus comes back receiving
   His bride

(Chorus 3x)

No more pain

. . . *from the album, point of grace* . . . .

NO MORE PAIN. Words and music by Geoff Thurman,
Becky Thurman & Michael English ©1993 P.E. Velvet
Music (a div. of the Harding Music Group)/Seventh Son
Music (a div. of the Glen Campbell Music Group)
(ASCAP)/Dayspring Music (a div. of Word, Inc.)(BMI)

It's funny

that my surroundings are

exactly the same when

I am afraid and when I'm

not. . . . The only

difference is me.

Terry Jones

. . . . . $\mathcal{N}$obody likes pain. When it comes, we all wish it away.

Several people I am especially close to are experiencing physical pain right now. My mom has had several scares with possible breast cancer. She's had many biopsies and has to visit the oncologist regularly. The doctors tell her she has a 95 percent chance of developing breast cancer. She is so brave and has such a positive attitude, but I know the unknown possibilities are difficult to live with. Some of my aunts also have had breast cancer. Seeing them in pain hurts me too.

Chris's dad, my father-in-law, has had renal cell cancer for years. He's had four lung and kidney surgeries, and he's completed interluken chemotherapy. We thank God that he is now in remission, but he's experienced so much pain during all of this. I know that sometimes he grows weary from dealing with it all.

Just recently, my Gramma Lang-Fugate passed away. Before her death she had undergone heart bypass surgery and then pneumonia. She knew a lot of pain in her last days. As my dad watched her suffer, he suffered too. My Grampa Drury has autonomic syndrome, which causes his blood pressure to drop, and he sometimes passes out. The last time he had an episode, he fell and broke his shoulder. Though his therapy worked wonders, it was hard for him to deal with the pain.

It's hard not to get angry when such great and giving people hurt so badly. I hate pain. I hate how it incapacitates people, how it drains them of energy. I hate how it discourages and wears down. Physical pain affects more than our bodies; it wounds our emotions and it wearies our spirits. I don't want to depress you about the amount of sickness and pain all around us; I just want to remind myself and you that, for Christians, *pain will end*. God promises us a refuge, a place where there is "no more pain." When I sing that song on stage, I think of those I love who are hurting. Even though I am sad for their pain, I am happy because I know it is only for a season.

Besides the hope of heaven, God also teaches us how to deal with the pain while we're here on earth. Colossians 3:2

says, "Set your minds on things above, not on earthly things." When we deal with pain, fear, anxiety, or anything that worries us, God wants us to "distract" our minds by thinking on "things above." He wants us to think about our home with him, his power, and his protection. He wants us to be aware of the spiritual realm.

This distraction "technique" also works with fear and worry. My husband, Chris, works for a private airline company, and he's often away from home. When he's gone, I sometimes get scared. I even get a little mad thinking about how unsafe our world is, and I wish for the days of unlocked doors and safety in our cities, and I worry—I worry that fear will be a big part of life for Cole and our children to come. I worry that someday we won't be safe even in our own home.

I have found, however, that if I keep myself busy, I forget to be afraid. If I can just distract myself from what scares me, I'm totally fine. I don't watch scary movies or the news. Instead, I clean the house, pay bills, write letters, pack for my next road trip, or most important, spend time with Cole. It's funny. My surroundings are exactly the same when I am afraid and when I'm not. The house has the same walls, the same yard, and is in the same neighborhood. The only thing that's different is me. When my mind is on other things, I'm not afraid.

I see this approach being used by the people I love to deal with pain. They distract their minds from their pain by focusing on other things, higher things—things above. My mom, in addition to giving love to her four girls, distracts her mind by working with hurting people in prison. She helps them find the heaven that fills her with hope. Chris's dad, although the CEO of a large company, finds joy in being distracted by his five grandchildren, whom he loves so dearly. And Grampa Drury loves playing the bass fiddle. He can leave all his worries and cares behind when he props it up to play. All of them have learned the secret of focusing on things beyond their pain.

Pain is a very real part of this life. Satan makes sure of that. He brings into our lives pain of all sorts—physical pain, emotional pain, relationship pain. He knows that when we are in pain, we might blame God, we might get discouraged, we might lash out and try to hurt others, we might lose our faith. But we know that we are headed for a place where there is no more pain, where there is no more sorrow, no more waiting, no more dying, no more striving or strain. If we will think on these things, even though our pain or environment may not change, our perspective will. The pain we suffer here on earth becomes bearable because we know it will end and we know that the joy of heaven will last for eternity.

God chooses to heal many sicknesses here on earth. And I praise God for those healings. You probably know some people personally who have been healed, but you also know some who have not. Perhaps you yourself are experiencing pain and see no relief in sight. Hang in there. Know that there will be no pain in heaven. There is hope for the future. Pray for those around you who are ill, pray for yourself if you are hurting, and know, without a doubt, that you can look forward to a place "where there will be no more pain, no more sorrow, no more waiting for illusive tomorrows."

The length of time we spend on this earth is just a flash compared to eternity. Whatever problems we have here are short-lived. And even while we live on this earth, there is so much more to life than what we can see with our eyes. May we all learn to be "distracted" in him.

questions

1. What pain is in your life or the life of someone you love?
2. What helps you be "distracted" from your fears?
3. What pain or fear do you most want to be rid of?
4. How does thinking on heaven give you a different perspective on pain?

. . . . *God of heaven,*

Please distract me from my fears and pain and point my eyes toward you. Teach me to see with spiritual eyes the realities of the heavenly realm. Let me rest in your care and protection for me and for those I love.

twenty-one

i have no doubt . . . . .

Immediately Jesus

reached out his hand

and caught him.

"You of little faith,"

he said, "why did

you doubt?"

—Matthew 14:31

Sometimes I don't know where I'm going
Where the road is leading me
Life can be full of so many changes
So many uncertainties
But there's one thing that's constant in this
    heart of mine
It's knowing that You're gonna love me,
    come rain or shine

(Chorus)
I have no doubt
That You will never leave me
That You'll be there to keep me safe and
    warm

. . . . . . *i have no doubt* . . . . . .

No matter where You take me
That nothing can separate me from
    You, Lord

I don't know what You've planned for
    tomorrow
Or what lies up ahead for me
Pleasure, pain, worry, or sorrow
Today is as far as I can see
You may see fit to take me through the
    valley, Lord
Or on the mountain. It makes no difference
    where I go

(Chorus)

(Bridge)
I wanna run away
From that voice that I hear calling
But I'll be quick to answer and obey

(Chorus)

Nothing could separate me
Nothing could ever separate me

. . . . from the album, point of grace . . . .

I HAVE NO DOUBT. Words by Dawn Thomas, music by
Tommy Greer ©1993 McSpadden Music (BMI)/ Word
Music (a div. of Word, Inc.) (ASCAP)

The minute I take my eyes off my Savior, I lose my source of strength and my faith is shaken.

Heather Floyd

. . . . . *N*ot long ago, my sister Misti was shopping at a store in Colorado Springs where she lives. It was about three in the afternoon, and she was struggling to carry her shopping bags under one arm and her seven-month-old son Mitch (the love of my life) in the other. Out of nowhere, a car pulled up beside the curb. A guy jumped out of the car, grabbed her purse, jumped back in the car, and sped off. She was helpless. There was nothing she could do to stop him. She and Mitch were unhurt, but she had been violated because she was vulnerable.

That's just how Satan works.

A precious friend of mine, Beth Moore, who wrote the Bible study I'm currently working on, describes Satan as a kidnapper. She said, "Kidnapping takes place when someone steals a person who belongs to another." The enemy is always on the lookout to catch faithful Christians in a weak moment. He waits until we are vulnerable, then he attacks. He chooses times when we are confused and full of fear.

Do you remember the time Jesus walked on water? I love this story from Matthew 14. Jesus had spoken to a crowd of about 5,000 people, then he sent his disciples ahead of him on a boat, while he went up on a mountainside to pray. It eventually got dark and Jesus was all alone. The disciples were already a good distance away from the shore when Jesus finished praying. But not having a boat didn't stop Jesus. He just stepped out on that lake and began to walk right on top of the water. When the disciples saw him walking on the water, they thought he was a ghost. Isn't that what you'd think if you saw a distant shape walking on top of the water in the middle of the night? The Bible says they were so terrified that they cried out in fear. Ahhhhh!

But firm assurance came quickly, "Take courage. It is I. Don't be afraid."

Now, Peter—impetuous Peter—wanted proof that it really was Jesus and not a ghost. "Lord, if it's really you, then tell me to come to you on the water." And Jesus simply replied, "Come."

And Peter, without thinking of the winds and waves, stepped boldly onto the water. He fearlessly moved forward, one step after the other. But then Peter suddenly became aware of his surroundings, and he got scared—scared of the seen and the unseen. He felt the force of the wind and saw the foam of the waves, and they frightened him so much that he took his eyes off Jesus. And that's when he became vulnerable. And that's when he began to sink.

I don't know about you, but I can really identify with Peter. So many times I sense the presence of Jesus and I really want to be where he is, to walk with him and be like him. And sometimes I actually do it. Those wonderful times when I really focus on God and don't feel compelled to make sense of my surroundings, I follow blindly. I take a step of faith—a step into the unknown. I move toward Jesus. I have him in my sights. But then, just when I'm about to experience something life changing, I freeze. I get so scared, and just like Peter, I'm flooded with doubt and fear. The minute I take my eyes off my Savior, I lose my source of strength and my faith is shaken. As believers, this is a very scary place to be.

When our focus shifts from God to the world, we become weak and open to a fall. Like Peter, we take our eyes off of Jesus. But our Lord never blinks an eye as he reaches out his hand to rescue us. He looks at us with knowing compassion and says, "Oh, you of little faith! Why did you doubt?"

The next time Jesus calls you to walk to him on the water, lock your eyes securely on his, refuse to look at the waves around you, and step out of your secure little boat onto the water. Take one step and then another—never taking your eyes off him. And then . . . if you do get scared and start looking at the waves and feeling the force of the wind and begin to sink, be assured that he will reach out his hand and rescue you.

Has he ever given me any reason to doubt? No, never. Not once. Yet, time and time again, I do. As far as I'm concerned, I'm a failure. As far as he's concerned, I am an heir of the Kingdom of God. Make sense? Not at all. But then again, that's what living with mystery is all about. "Now we see in a mirror dimly, but one day . . ."

questions

1. Have you even been violated at a time when you were vulnerable? What happened? How did you feel?
2. How does Beth Moore's definition of kidnapping apply to how Satan tries to work in our lives?
3. Have you ever had an experience like Peter when you were beginning to walk out in faith but got scared and sank? Did you call out to Jesus for help? If not, how do you think things would have been different if you had?

. . . . . . *Father,*

I come before you with my little seed of faith and ask you to help it grow. I know that you are the source of all growth, and I believe you can help my faith grow. Next time you call upon me to step out in faith, help me to keep my eyes locked onto yours and to keep walking. And if I do falter, Father, be gracious to me—as you always are—and rescue me once again.

twenty-two

drawing me closer . . . . . .

But I, when I am

lifted up from the

earth, will draw all

men to myself.

—John 12:32

I'd be lost here inside myself
I'd be nothing without You
If your ways didn't pull me in
Like they do

(Chorus)
It's the hope I know, the grace You
   show
That's drawing me closer, drawing me
   closer
It's the peace I feel, it's Your love so real
That's drawing me closer, drawing
   me closer
And my heart beats with pure amazement
Every time I feel the tender touch of
   Your love

. . . . . . drawing me closer . . . .

Tell me how when You hold me near
I can feel so free
Where would I be if not for You
Moving me

(Chorus)
Your love . . .

(Bridge)
I can hear Your voice it's calling me
To the shelter of Your arms

200

(Chorus)
It's the hope I know, the grace You show
That's drawing me closer
It's the peace I feel, it's Your love so real
That's drawing me closer

(1st Chorus)

Your love . . . drawing me closer, closer, closer
Hey, hey now
Hear Your voice it's calling me
Hey, hey now
Drawing me closer

. . . . *from the album, steady on* . . . .

Hey, hey now
Everybody come and see
Hey, hey now yeah
Drawing me closer
Hey, hey now

While it surely hurts him

when we ignore him,

God is a faithful Friend

and Father.

Denise Jones

. . . . *H*ave you ever thought about what draws you to certain people? Is it their good looks, their charming personality? Money? Power? Maybe at first. But for me, and probably for you, what continues to draw me to get to know someone is much more than what's on the surface. It starts with common interests, and then it expands to how they make you feel and what's in their hearts.

I remember when I met my husband Stu for the first time. He was cute and seemed confident and charming—in his own way. When he called and asked me out, I was interested enough to take a chance and go on a date. We went to eat pizza and play Putt-Putt. There I found out that we both loved sports, liked to laugh, and were both very competitive.

As time when on, I was drawn to know him beyond those things. I found that he was sweet and sensitive, strong but not overbearing. He made me feel safe, and he truly cared for me. I could go on and on, but I'll spare you the gushy stuff.

When I went away to college, there were long stretches of time between visits. Every now and then, another guy would catch my eye, and the idea of having someone there, nearby, was somewhat appealing. At times, I wondered if this guy back in Oklahoma was worth the effort of a long-distance relationship. Now, Stu says I was just fickle. Thank goodness he continued to pursue me and show me how much he cared about me. I finally came around and realized that I truly loved him and wanted to spend the rest of my life with him.

Have you ever felt fickle toward God? Do you know what I mean? Some days, I think he's the greatest thing in my life and I don't know what I would do without him. Other days—especially when it's been a while since I've had some really good, quality time with him, I can't feel much of a spark. One week, maybe even two or three, can pass before I realize how long it's been since I've spoken to him. But the amazing thing about God is that even when I lag behind in our relationship, he never lets me go.

I was talking to my dear friend Rose Ann the other day, and I was telling her how busy I'd been and how guilty I felt because I hadn't even opened my Bible for a week. I was feeling distant from God. The longer I stayed away, the more awkward I felt. I was hesitant to approach him for fear he was mad at me. You know how you feel when you haven't called a friend in a long time? When you finally think about calling, you feel weird because it's been so long. That, I told Rose Ann, was how I felt toward God.

But Rose Ann reminded me that God is always anxious to hear from us. While it surely hurts him when we ignore him, he is a faithful Friend and Father. There is nothing fickle about him. Even when I don't hold up my end of the relationship, he remains constant. He loves me. And he loves you. He has so much to share with us that he can't wait for us to pick up the phone and call.

And the amazing thing is that he doesn't always wait for me to call. He actually does the dialing! As the song says, he continues to draw us closer to him by the grace he shows, by the peace he puts in our hearts. He insists on loving us, even when we drift away from him.

These are the traits of God that we are drawn to, or perhaps I should say that he uses to draw us to himself.

questions

1. Who is your best friend? What is it that draws you to him or her?
2. Have you ever been fickle in a relationship with a friend? Has a friend ever been fickle toward you? How did you or your friend respond?
3. Have you ever had a friend or family member who continued to pursue a relationship with you even when you didn't hold up your end? Have you ever been the "pursuer" in such a relationship? What did you learn from those experiences?
4. What is it about God that draws you to him? How does God draw you to himself even when you neglect the relationship?

most gracious heavenly Father,

Thank you for continually showing yourself to me even when I am not so faithful to you. Develop in me a hunger to be with you so strong that I can't stay away. And in the meantime, while you're growing that hunger in me, help me discipline myself to come to you on a regular basis to be fed. I praise you for the grace you've given me so freely. I thank you for the peace you put in my heart. I exalt your steadfast love.

twenty-three

the love he has for you . . .

See that no one is sexually

immoral, or is godless like

Esau, who for a single

meal sold his inheritance

rights as the oldest son.

—Hebrews 12:16

When you're living for the love of
  a lifetime
You wonder if the waiting will ever end
And the right from the wrong
That you've guarded so long
Is closer than it's ever been
But sometimes a moment of weakness
Can sacrifice the treasures of time
And cause you to miss the miracle
That God longs for you to find

(Chorus)
There's a love He has for you
There's a heart that He's been saving
There's a joy beyond all measure
That only comes from waiting
There's a love He has for you
It's more than the hope you're holding to
And you will find the only love that's true
Is . . .

. . . the love he has for you . . . .

When you're torn between today
  and tomorrow
And holding out for something you
  cannot see
There's a strength you can find
Knowing in God's own time
You'll discover what He meant to be
'Cause love like the Father intended
Is more than just a state of the heart
So don't give up hope in the holding on
'Cause no matter who you are

(Chorus)

. . . from the album, the whole truth . . . .

Don't let a weak moment

take away something

you can never

get back.

Shelley Breen

a bstinence—most people these days think this is an archaic term, something that doesn't apply to this generation. We happen to believe otherwise. God calls each of us to live a life set apart and different from those outside the body of Christ, a life of purity in every way, a holy life.

One of the neatest things the four of us girls have in common is our decision in junior high to save sex for marriage. I didn't realize then the impact that decision would have on my future. I just figured it was probably the right thing to do. At the time, I didn't even know that God's Word gives us specific instructions about this matter.

I know that in this day and age, saving sex for marriage is not an easy or popular thing to do. We are surrounded by TV shows and movies that show sex as a natural part of a "love" (or more often than not, a "like") relationship. It's as if sex is a given; there is little or no consideration as to whether it is a right or wrong issue.

I remember being so infuriated once while watching the TV show, *Friends*. Rachel and Monica, two roommates on the show, were having their boyfriends spend the night and there was a fight over who got to use the last condom in the drawer of the girls' bathroom. The issue was not "Is premarital sex right or wrong?" but "What are we going to do about birth control?" I sat there in disbelief, wondering how teenage viewers would ever get the whole truth. You see, TV shows like this make premarital sex the absolute norm. In essence, the world is lying to our young people.

Teens and singles, please remember that your body belongs to the Lord, not to some guy or girl, no matter how much you think you love him or her. I implore you to wait. Make the decision now. And if you've already had premarital sex, confess it to God, ask him to forgive you, and commit to purity from this day forward until marriage. Some teenagers think that once they've lost their virginity, they can no longer be pure in God's eyes, so why even try to abstain from now on. But Christianity is all about second chances. That's what grace is. You can determine to be pure from this day forward, and you can know that you will be pure and clean in God's eyes.

I could give you many reasons to make this decision, but the most important one is simple: It's the right way because it's God's way. God's Word is clear in it's teachings to save sex for the covenant of marriage:

> Let us behave decently, as in the daytime, not in orgies and drunkenness, not in sexual immorality and debauchery, not in dissension and jealousy. (Rom. 13:13)

> The body is not meant for sexual immorality, but for the Lord, and the Lord for the body. (1 Cor. 6:13)

> Flee from sexual immorality. All other sins a man commits are outside his body, but he who sins sexually sins against his own body. (1 Cor. 6:18)

> But among you there must not be even a hint of sexual immorality, or of any kind of impurity, or of greed, because these are improper for God's holy people. (Eph. 5:3)

> See that no one is sexually immoral, or is godless like Esau, who for a single meal sold his inheritance rights as the oldest son. (Heb. 12:16)

I think the last verse is my favorite because it so graphic. God is telling us here that when we give ourselves sexually before we are married, we are exchanging our precious virginity for a *bowl of beans!* Think about that the next time you are tempted to give away your purity.

Have faith and know that God has a love just for you. But what do you do in the meantime, in the lonely times? Let me challenge you to pursue God rather than a boyfriend or girlfriend. The love and peace that he brings is so much more fulfilling than any person will ever be. Please don't misunderstand me. Marriage is a wonderful adventure. The first year of my marriage has been a blast. I love being married because I believe David is the love God had chosen for me. And I am so thankful that on my wedding day I had the peace of knowing that I had waited. David was worth the wait.

Don't let a weak moment take away something you can never get back. I believe that if you stay out of situations that could turn out to be compromising, God will reward you with great relationships. Do you trust God with your future? If you do, then don't give in to the ways of the world.

When a high school girl from Nashville was asked why she was waiting to have sex until marriage, she replied, "I want my future husband to know I loved him even before I knew him." That all teenagers would be able to say the same—what a precious thing in God's sight.

questions

1. What messages do you hear from the world regarding sex? How are these messages different from what God wants for you?
2. What reasons can you think of to abstain from sex until marriage?
3. How can you handle the loneliness that sometimes occurs while you wait?
4. Have you saved sex for marriage thus far? If so, will you renew your commitment to remain pure? If not, will you confess your sin to God and commit to be pure from this day forward?

. . . . . *God of purity,*

Thank you for giving us the intimacy and beauty of the sexual relationship. I commit to keep myself sexually pure from this day forward. Guard me from sexual temptation, and if temptation comes, please give me the courage to take the way out that you have promised to provide. I praise you for being a God of second chances. I commit my body to you today.

twenty-four

the house that mercy built . . .

In all their distress he too was
distressed, and the angel of his
presence saved them. In his love
and mercy he redeemed them;
he lifted them up and carried
them all the days of old.

—Isaiah 63:9

A light in the distance
Welcomes those wayfaring souls
Come this far
A heart grows tired, faith grows cold
Wandering down the winding road
Just simply knock, the door will open

There is a house that mercy built
There is a place where brokeness is
    healed
There is a voice saying peace be still
There is a house that mercy built
Mercy will find you
Though you've given up
In the middle of what seems like nowhere
He'll shelter you beneath His wing
His love will cover every need
Just simply seek and you will find

There is a

. . . . *house that mercy built* . . . .

There is a place where emptiness is filled
There is a voice saying peace be still
There is a house that mercy built

There is a house that mercy built
With blood and tears
We've nothing left to fear
We live in grace
Here in the safe embrace of God
The mercy of God

There is a house that mercy built
There is a place where grace has
  been revealed
There is a voice saying peace be still
There is a house that mercy built
Rest in the hope
Rest in the peace
There is a house that mercy built

. . . . *from the album, the whole truth* . . . . . .

God's mercy

· ·

is yours for the asking.

Terry Jones

.　.　.　.　.　.　. *O*ne sunny day in Monroe, Louisiana, I was changed.

We were scheduled to go to a girls' home for the afternoon and evening. The plan was that we would have dinner with the girls and then sing for them. Simple enough. We knew how to eat, and we knew how to sing. The evening shouldn't present anything out of the ordinary—nothing we couldn't handle.

We knew Mercy Ministries of America took girls in and helped them, but we had no idea how much the power of God in their lives would affect us. From what we'd been told, these girls knew about the ugly side of life. They had been abused by the people who were supposed to love them. Many were pregnant and had made the difficult, sacrificial decision to carry their babies to full term, rather than having an abortion. We were a little nervous about the visit, though I'm not sure why. Maybe we thought that girls who had been through so much pain and heartache would be hard and apathetic. Maybe we didn't think we could identify with them since we had been sheltered from the kind of pain they knew. Whatever the reason, there was no need.

When we walked in the front door of Mercy Ministries, we instantly knew that God was at work there. We were greeted by two enthusiastic teenage girls and by Nancy Alcorn, the founder and director of Mercy Ministries. Then we were taken on a tour of the home. As we went from room to room, our little entourage grew, as each girl we met joined us on our tour. Soon, we had a whole group of girls buzzing around us like little bees. After our tour, we sat down to a wonderful meal. The girls had made it especially for us and were so cute and proud of their meal—spaghetti, salad, and bread—and it was delicious!

After we ate, Nancy asked us to introduce ourselves and tell the girls a little about ourselves. That was easy. Then she asked the girls to introduce themselves, one by one, and tell us where they were from and why they were here. And with surprising openness, each girl told her story. One smiling young girl, named Janice, showed us pictures of what she looked like before she came to Mercy Ministries. She looked almost dead, without hope, without color. She had been sexually abused and was burdened by heavy guilt. But when she started applying what she learned at Mercy about God's love, her whole life became new. Another girl, a twenty-two year old red head named Andrea, told us she came to Mercy Ministries when she found herself pregnant and with no way to support a child. At Mercy, she came to know God and made the difficult decision to parent her baby herself. Her life continues to be one testimony for God's power after another. As I listened to these amazing stories of courage and grace, my eyes filled with tears. I looked around at Heather, Shelley, and Denise and saw that they were crying too. By the time all the girls had shared their stories, the four of us were wrecks from crying.

It had been our plan to minister to the girls in the home, but instead we were ministered to by them. Their hopeful hearts, their spirit of cooperation and camaraderie, and their acceptance of God's mercy touched my heart in ways I will never forget. I was forever changed.

Besides being blessed by the hope and promise we saw in these girls, we were also blessed to see the amazing power of God to change an individual life. They shared with us how God was teaching them so much at Mercy. They told us they had found love there. God had healed each individual girl from her painful past and given her a future filled with hope and promise.

We talk about Mercy Ministries in our concerts because we've seen the power of God's mercy to change lives firsthand. We believe in what is happening there. This ministry is the only one we've joined hands with to help on a full-time basis. It's good to know that the grace and forgiveness of Christ is being acted out in real ways. Nancy Alcorn may have founded Mercy, but God continues to provide a way out for these girls. In addition to the two homes in Monroe, in 1995 Mercy Ministries opened a two-million-dollar, fifty-bed facility in Nashville—debt free! They presently have properties ready to build on in Los Angeles, Houston, and near Washington D.C. Their work of mercy extends even beyond the United States. They currently have an administrative office in Australia and are laying plans to build a home there and are in the preliminary stages of building a home in Great Britain. God has provided miraculously for their tremendous financial needs. Simply clothing, feeding, and getting Christian teaching supplies costs a tremendous amount of money. It has been a blessing to see the conscientious stewardship of those who handle the funds in Mercy Ministries.

God is in the business of changing lives. He's changing the lives of the girls in the House of Mercy and he can change yours too. Think on the beautiful words from this passage in the book of Psalms:

> Hear, O Lord, and be merciful to me;
>> O Lord, be my help.
> You turned my wailing into dancing;
>> you removed my sackcloth and clothed me
>>> with joy,
> that my heart may sing to you and not be silent.

O Lord my God, I will give you thanks for
ever. (Psalm 30:10–12)

Have you ever cried so much you thought you'd never stop? This passage says that God will turn your tears into dancing. Have you ever felt so sad it seemed you were *wearing* your sadness? God will clothe you in joy instead. Has your heart ever felt so burdened that you couldn't even speak? God will fill your mouth with song. God's mercy is yours for the asking. He loves you and wants to bring healing to your life.

As you probably know, healing takes time. Just like the girls at Mercy Ministries were not healed overnight, you, too, will need time to heal. But that healing can begin right now. Help and healing come from all kinds of sources. Maybe you need to go to God in prayer and open your heart to His healing mercy. Or perhaps you need to talk with someone, like your parents or a pastor or a trusted friend. Or maybe you need the kind of help Mercy Ministries can give. If you need to make a phone call, do it now. If you need to seek God's spiritual healing through prayer, stop right now and talk to Him.

As the song says, "There is a place where brokenness is healed; there is a voice saying peace be still. There is a house that mercy built." The doors of that house are open wide for you. Come on in.

Mercy Ministries Special Help Line: 800-922-9131
All other inquiries: 615-831-6987
 or write: Mercy Ministries of America, PO Box 111060,
 Nashville, TN 37222-1060

questions

1. Have you ever seen the work of God in someone else's life in such a way that it changed your life too? Describe that experience and how it changed you.
2. When was the last time you felt desperate and in need of help? Why did you feel this way? Where did you go for help? Did you go to the right source?
3. Describe a time when someone extended mercy and healing to you.
4. Describe a time when you extended mercy and healing to someone else.
5. Is God's mercy and healing at work in you right now? How?

. . . . *God of mercy,*

Come in to the empty, broken places in my heart and restore them with your touch of mercy. Thank you that you are a merciful God and that you use your power and strength to heal and not to harm. Teach me to extend mercy and healing to other hurting souls. Open my eyes to see their pain. I praise you for your steadfast mercy and love.